P9-BAW-318

WITHDRAWN

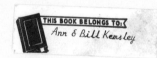

THIS BOOK BELONGS TO:
Ann & Bill Kemsley

WITHDRAWN

Report from Wasteland

"The Weapons Don't Work So Well, But The Costs Are Over-Running Right On Schedule"

Copyright 1969 by Herblock in *The Washington Post*

Report from Wasteland

AMERICA'S MILITARY-INDUSTRIAL COMPLEX

SENATOR WILLIAM PROXMIRE

FOREWORD BY
Senator Paul H. Douglas

WITHDRAWN

PRAEGER PUBLISHERS
New York · Washington · London

To two gallant public servants,
A. E. Fitzgerald and John McGee,
in the hope that
their courage may help
build a stronger America

PRAEGER PUBLISHERS
111 Fourth Avenue, New York, N.Y. 10003, U.S.A.
5, Cromwell Place, London S.W.7, England

Published in the United States of America in 1970
by Praeger Publishers, Inc.

Second printing, 1970

© 1970 by Praeger Publishers, Inc.

All rights reserved

Library of Congress Catalog Card Number: 72–95687

Printed in the United States of America

Contents

v

Foreword

EVERYONE INTERESTED in public affairs should read this book. It shows with solid evidence how we are wasting at least $10 billion a year on our weapons systems. Until Senator Proxmire began his investigations less than two years ago, this field was treated as "off limits" as far as congressional scrutiny was concerned. Because the subject was highly technical as well as crucial to physical and national security, Congress deprived itself of any adequate means of finding out what was going on.

Following urgings and exposures in 1959–60 by our inquiries on the Joint Economic Committee into the purchase and use of common civilian items, Secretary of Defense Robert S. McNamara instituted a thoroughgoing program of reform in this field. His action saved several billion dollars a year and stamped the Secretary as the ablest and most public-spirited government administrator for many years.

However, just as I had done as Chairman of the Joint Economic Committee, Secretary McNamara postponed going into weapons procurement until he could carry through his reforms in the less controversial field. Perhaps he was also influenced by his experience with the TFX (F-111) plane, which he first sponsored and which, after prolonged trial, seems to have been proved a gigantic error. Moreover, after 1963 the Vietnam war increasingly absorbed his attention. Whatever the complex of reasons, he did not control prime contracts and weapons procurement. They now comprise about half of our huge military costs, or about $40 billion a year, or one-quarter of our total federal expenditures.

Thus, both Congress and the executive branch of the U.S. Government allowed the military to run wild without challenge.

Senator Proxmire has penetrated the wall of secrecy surrounding weapons procurement and, with the aid of a devoted and able staff, has thrown the white light of publicity upon some of the costs of the "military-industrial complex" that President Dwight D. Eisenhower feared and against which he tried to warn the American people in his Farewell Address.

This book is the thrilling account of Proxmire's investigations as chairman of the Economy in Government Subcommittee. Beginning with the C-5A cargo plane, Proxmire discovered that the actual costs of the plane were not the $3.37 billion authorized but would be at least $1.9 billion more, or $5.33 billion. Further inquiry revealed that this overrun of actual costs was the rule rather than the exception. Despite the strenuous efforts of the military to cover it up, some of the truth came tumbling out.

In particular, the courageously accurate testimony of the Air Force expert A. E. Fitzgerald helped expose the facts. He was rewarded for his public spirit by dismissal. Much the same treatment was meted out to another civic hero, John

McGee. It is impossible not to feel indignant at the punishment they suffered for doing their duty.

In the course of his investigations, Proxmire found out the submarine rescue vehicle had experienced an even greater expansion of cost than the C-5A. Originally authorized at an outlay of $36 million for twelve vehicles, the price skyrocketed to $460 million for only six of them, an increase of from $3 million to $77 million per unit, or twenty-five times. In addition, the total cost of the strategic missile (Minutemen I and II, with Minuteman III to come) will expand from $3 billion to $7 billion.

An assistant to McNamara has said that the ultimate cost of a weapons system is, in 90 per cent of the cases, double the original estimate, and another expert says that the typical cost overrun is from 300 per cent to 700 per cent.

Proxmire punctures the usual excuses for such excesses. He proves that inflation was a relatively minor cause and that, if improvements in design were a factor, they were relatively ineffective. Of thirteen aircraft and missile systems with electronic equipment begun since 1955, only four, costing $5 billion, were as much as 75 per cent effective. Five more, costing $13 billion, broke down at a performance level 75 per cent or less of that fixed in the contract. Two more systems, costing $10 billion, were dropped after a time because of "low reliability." Finally, the contracts for two systems were canceled. Their cost was $2 billion.

It is characteristic of Senator Proxmire that he is not only accurate in revealing the personnel and companies in the "military-industrial complex" but also fair-minded in his treatment of them. He makes no charges of wholesale corruption, contenting himself with disclosing the shameful record of deception, incompetence, and cover-up. He proposes a modest program of reform, which would greatly reduce the waste.

He shows that the number of former high-ranking officers

in the employ of the 100 most important defense firms is over 2,100, or three times the number I found a decade earlier, and he traces the positions they occupy, making the complex resemble a series of revolving doors. I had at my side in my investigations an extremely competent assistant, Howard Shuman, and it is a pleasure to know that he is similarly associated with Senator Proxmire.

The companies in the arms complex are easily identified. Fifteen of them get one-third of all prime weapons contracts. They are Lockheed, General Electric, General Dynamics, McDonnell Douglas, United Aircraft, American Telephone and Telegraph, Ling-Temco-Vought, North American Rockwell, Boeing, General Motors, Raytheon, Sperry Rand, AVCO, Hughes Aircraft, and Westinghouse Electric.

Senator Proxmire has done much; he will do more. I am afraid, however, that the complex will try to do to him and his staff what it has already done to Fitzgerald. If this happens, congressional criticism will be choked off or curtailed. The American people cannot allow this to occur. They are now being put to the test. It remains to be seen whether they will take the trouble to defend both themselves and their real protectors. We can only hope.

PAUL H. DOUGLAS

Preface

THIS BOOK is about cost overruns and military waste. Even while it was being printed, a number of events took place that affect its substance.

The immediate results of the fight we made against military waste and excessive spending have been far more successful than most of us imagined. In a move little publicized and almost unknown to the general public, Congress cut $8 billion from President Johnson's original military budget request for fiscal 1970 and $5.6 billion from the revised budget request submitted by President Nixon.

This was done over the initial vigorous objections of President Nixon, who referred to those leading the fight as the "new isolationists," and the Secretary of Defense, who claimed the cuts would harm our security. Nonetheless, shortly after the cuts were made, those who resisted them most strenuously sought credit as their progenitors.

Basically, what Congress did was to reorder priorities. It cut ten appropriations bills by $7.6 billion ($6 billion of which was in the military and military construction bills). It increased funds on four bills by $2 billion (of which $1.1 billion was for education and health). The result was an overall or net reduction of $5.6 billion.

In addition, cuts in the number of military and civilian Defense Department personnel have been announced to take place over an eighteen-month period. Provided this is well planned, it can result in releasing manpower and resources, now used for relatively inefficient purposes, for highly productive ones. Military personnel would be reduced from 3.4 million to about 2.8 million, still well above the pre-Vietnam levels. Civilian Pentagon workers would be cut by 150,000 in eighteen months. This should cause no real hardship, for there is a Pentagon turnover of about 20,000 employees a month, or 360,000 in eighteen months, who routinely resign or retire. These are welcome moves and a good beginning.

Other things have happened, too. Not only did Senator Thomas J. McIntyre and his Armed Services Subcommittee make a substantial cut in the authorization for military research and development, but the effect of the fight by Senator J. William Fulbright and the amendment by Senator Mike Mansfield was to outlaw Pentagon research and development contracts not directly related to military matters. If the letter and spirit of the Mansfield amendment are carried out, not only will a substantial cut in military spending take place, but also military influence will be vastly reduced in areas where it does not belong. This little-noticed fight may be one of the most significant events in helping to return control of the military to civilian authorities.

Shortly after my amendment to cut back the number of C-5A airplanes was defeated, the Air Force itself announced it would build only 81 of the 120 projected. There is a lesson in this. Under pressure from public opinion, Pentagon officials will take actions on their own that they resist violently when proposed by others. Thus, although they organized a crushing defeat for my Senate floor amendment, much of its purpose was accomplished almost immediately thereafter. Even the Pentagon gives way to informed criticism and legitimate fiscal pressures. That is why it is so necessary to keep pressing for change.

While these actions are welcome, there are still many discouraging aspects. The cuts in the C-5A, for example, represent no increase in efficiency or productivity. The 81 planes will cost as much as the estimates for the original 120. Thus, for 39 fewer planes, we will spend at least the same amount of money as originally allotted. This is no real gain or improvement in the system. All it means, to use the vernacular, is "less bang for a buck."

Furthermore, although the Air Force throughout 1969 repeatedly denied before my Subcommittee that there had been any reduction in the physical standards for the C-5A, the plane was, nevertheless, grounded when a crack appeared in the wing. We had previously brought out that the plane had failed to meet the initial wing-stress standards.

The superb testimony by the General Accounting Office (GAO) before the Economy in Government Subcommittee in late December, 1969, established that the cost overruns for 38 major weapons systems had increased by at least $20 billion, or by 50 per cent. Furthermore, Assistant Comptroller General Robert K. Keller testified that no one person or central agency at the Pentagon knew the total number of major weapons systems being acquired or their cost. This testimony by an impeccable independent source confirmed and re-enforced the work of our Subcommittee and the criticisms of weapons-systems procurement that we had made for over a year. While it is often pleasant to be proved right, especially after the denials and pressures from what is called the military-industrial complex, it is discouraging for me, as a citizen and as a Senator, to know that weapons cost far too much, are delivered far too late, and function far below their specifications, which is what both the GAO and Navy testimony in our most recent hearings bore out.

Additionally, the General Accounting Office has released its study on uniform accounting standards in which it supports the need for them as well as the Subcommittee's and Admiral Rickover's judgment as to the savings that could be made if such a system were instituted.

Finally, it is discouraging to see how determined the Pentagon is to inflict revenge on anyone within the system who tries to save money or to bring reforms. After testifying truthfully before our Subcommittee, A. E. Fitzgerald was, in turn, ostracized, lied about, investigated, and fired.

Yet, while all this was being done, officialdom denied it. Secretary Seamans testified before my Subcommittee in November, 1969, that no investigation of Fitzgerald had taken place. But an investigation had been under way since May, 1969. It began only a few days after the Secretary himself alleged, quite wrongly, before a House Committee that A. E. Fitzgerald had leaked classified information to Congress.

After Fitzgerald was fired, the Secretary testified before my Subcommittee that Fitzgerald's job was cut merely to save money. At that point, the audience laughed. In the almost thirteen years I have been in the Senate, I have never witnessed a more embarrassing occasion.

The testimony on that day formed the basis on which I subsequently wrote to the Attorney General asking him to determine whether Title 18 of the U.S. Code had been violated. That section of the law makes it a criminal offense to influence, intimidate, or impede any witness in connection with any hearing before Congress on account of his testimony. It makes it a criminal offense to injure a person because he testified before Congress. Under the statutes, "injure" has been held to include removal from a job.

A. E. Fitzgerald was fired for his testimony. It is still to be determined whether the Justice Department will include the Pentagon in its crusade for law and order.

In any case, what the Pentagon does seem intent on proving is that it has no place for anyone determined to cut costs and stop military waste. The firing of A. E. Fitzgerald will discourage every free spirit who works for the government.

It mocks the original intent of the Civil Service system by making it a protection system for the time-servers. The Pentagon action portends a Kafkaesque bureaucracy composed of those who combine lethargy with servility in a feudalistic system.

Political democracy cannot function in that atmosphere.

There are several people I must thank for their help on this book. First, there is my Administrative Assistant, Howard E. Shuman. Shuman did all the research. He worked very closely with me on virtually every paragraph. He deserves more credit for the book, in most respects, than I do. Second, there is Lois O'Neill, of Praeger Publishers' Washington office, who proposed that I write this account. Finally, while unconnected with work on the book itself, Richard Kaufman deserves great credit for developing much of the critical evidence on the weapons systems. The public has little understanding of how significant a role even one staff man can play against the vast resources of the military bureaucracy. The Subcommittee on Economy in Government developed the evidence of military profligacy with the aid of only one full-time staff man. This is truly a David and Goliath tale.

I also want to mention Barbara R. Baugher, who typed and retyped the manuscript. Dave Wilson, who worked as an intern in my office, did the drudgery involved in indexing the book. They are owed my heartfelt thanks.

I

The Power of the Pentagon

MILITARY SPENDING in the United States is out of control.

The Department of Defense now spends nearly half of every federal tax dollar, or almost $80 billion last year. Yet there is no sufficiently critical review of what the Pentagon spends or of how it spends public monies, although these billions, however else one may regard them, are finally nothing more than hard-earned tax dollars—yours and mine.

There is, at present, no adequate machinery, in either the executive or the legislative branch, to control the total amount spent by the Pentagon or the way in which military funds are disbursed. This astonishing lack of supervision invites offenses, and they occur in all areas of military spending.

One of the most obvious offenses is the disproportionate amount of our resources the military services spend on marginal luxuries. This includes the maintenance of post exchanges, commissaries, ships' stores, officers' and noncommissioned officers' clubs, expensive jet planes assigned to generals who could travel by commercial airline on routine business, and similar items.

There is a great deal of fat, also, in the Pentagon-supported research and development programs—many of them only tenuously related to national defense needs—now being conducted on hundreds of campuses and in scores of DOD-spawned "think tanks."

But nowhere are the abuses of American tradition and the waste of our national resources greater than in the system of weapons procurement that has evolved out of the partnership between the Pentagon and the defense industry. Here, incredible inefficiency, extravagance, and covering-up of error have become the rule. And these abuses have created a situation in which we get less security for the country than we could by spending much smaller amounts more honestly and efficiently. Not only do we pay too much for the military hardware we buy. But, in addition, and far more shocking, we often do not get the weapons and products we pay for.

Time after time, important components of our weapons systems, or even whole systems themselves, do not meet the contract standards and specifications that were originally established for them. Instead of getting a plane, tank, or missile that can be depended upon to help safeguard the security of the country, we get huge cost increases, delayed deliveries, and far too many systems that are too faulty to deploy.

Among the most persistent and able critics of the Pentagon is one of its own, a senior U.S. Navy officer. Admiral Hyman Rickover is a doer as well as a critic. He is fighting for a strong, effective national security force. His words of criticism and warning deserve the broadest public notice.

Testifying before the Economy in Government Subcommittee of the Joint Economic Committee of the Senate and the House of Representatives in the summer of 1969, the Admiral called the laws covering defense contracting "toothless, loose, and outmoded." In the most sweeping indictment of Pentagon contracting of his career, he charged that the laws governing defense purchases are riddled with loopholes and need tightening and drastic overhaul and that the Pentagon is too much influenced by the industry viewpoint in procurement matters.

At the present time, it is not inaccurate or unfair to describe the U.S. weapons acquisition system as a kind of welfare system for the military brass and the DOD bureaucracy, on the one hand, and the top aerospace and munitions manufacturers, on the other. Instead of a defense production system geared to supply military needs with all possible dispatch and economy, we have a Pentagon procurement system that weakens, rather than strengthens, us. It saps our economic resources. It promotes inflation. It misuses our skilled manpower. It wastes the energies and genius of our engineers, scientists, and intellectuals, while technical and academic research is misdirected.

All this is the result of too much power in the hands of the military buyers and their civilian industrial friends—the biggest spenders the world has ever seen.

We could get far more defense for our money or the same defense for a great deal less money. A wide range of competent authorities believe that it is possible to make big savings in the defense budget without sacrificing miltary muscle.

Admiral Rickover testified before our Economy in Government Subcommittee that, by establishing uniform accounting standards for recording costs and profits, we could save "at least 5 per cent" of the defense procurement budget, which is $2 billion for that item alone.

Robert S. Benson, a former official of the Department of Defense, believes that $9 billion can be cut from the Pentagon budget. He wrote in the *Washington Monthly* (March, 1969) that this cut could be made "without reducing our national security or touching those funds earmarked for the war in Vietnam."

Earlier, the editors of the *Congressional Quarterly* interviewed highly placed sources at the Pentagon and in the defense industry about the defense budget. These were not outside critics but experts on the inside, whose narrow interests might be expected to render them uncritical. They, too, said that the Pentagon budget is loaded with fat. They set $10.8 billion as the figure we could cut without in the slightest way impairing our level of national defense.

Over the years, the American public has had highly ambivalent attitudes toward defense matters. As a result, national security policy has often seemed to ride a wild roller coaster. In the spirit of isolationism of the 1930's, despite the threats to world peace from Germany, Italy, and Japan, we starved our military services and placed the security of the country in deadly peril. At the end of World War II, we happily and overhastily dismantled a great military machine. Then, almost immediately, as a new and very real threat from the Soviet Union materialized, we again moved swiftly to build our defenses.

It was this threat that led us into a panicky and uncritical policy toward Pentagon spending and permitted the absence of adequate controls on contracts for new weapons systems. We overreacted. Nothing was too good for the military. Congress abandoned its critical reviews of defense spending. The Bureau of the Budget abdicated its oversight functions—leaving them to the Department of Defense itself. "Gold-plating" became the accepted and acceptable way of doing military business. During this period, Americans, in general, felt guilty when an occasional worrier raised questions about excessive spending or asked whether we were getting our money's worth. We gave a blank check to the military, the filling in of which has proved disastrous for both our security and the national economy.

Today, we have sufficient military might to create an atomic holocaust, but, at the same time, we are incapable of defeating relatively small guerrilla forces in the jungles of Asia.

In part, this is because no nation is omnipotent. The idea, which still persists among too many, that this country or any country can affect events outside its jurisdiction by a wave of the checkbook is both wrong and wrong-headed. The days of gunboats up the Yangtze are over.

But that we sometimes are a latter-day Gulliver tied down by Lilliputians is a result of military gold-plating. We have built tanks that do not work in the jungle; planes so complex they cannot function; guns and other weapons so fastidious that a team of mechanics and support troops is required to follow them around to keep them in repair, to fill out the forms to requisition new parts, or to initiate change orders for the manufacturer if the equipment proves ineffective in battle. At times, moreover, the Army, Navy, Air Force, and the nation's military contractors are so surfeited that we are unable to deploy the weapons they devised.

The *Pueblo* affair was symptomatic of this general situation. The forces to protect that U.S. Navy ship were said to be on alert and ready to defend it if necessary. But, as the testimony at the inquiry clearly showed, the forces supposed to be on call were not on call. For a period of about twenty-four hours after the initial attack took place, we were unable to bring to bear, even if we had desired to do so, the relatively small force from the military might of this country needed to protect that ship.

In a scathing seventy-seven-page report on the *Pueblo* capture, a Special House of Representatives Armed Services

Subcommittee said the incident and that of the EC-121 spy plane led to the inescapable conclusion that the military is "unable" to respond swiftly to a major crisis.

It concluded with these harsh words:

> The reluctant but inescapable conclusion finally reached by the Subcommittee is that because of the vastness of the military structure, with its complex division into multiple layers of command, and the failure of responsible authorities at the seat of Government to either delegate responsibility or in the alternative provide clear and unequivocal guidelines covering policy in emergency situations—our military command structure is now simply unable to meet the emergency criterion outlined and suggested by the President himself.

The *Pueblo* affair is to the military side of our national security problem what the C-5A, the Navy submarine-rescue-vehicle and the Minuteman overruns are to procurement and contracting. Each epitomizes our dilemma.

The cost of the C-5A giant attack cargo plane increased from $3.37 billion to over $5.33 billion, or almost $2 billion. The overrun was so big that Congress might very well have changed its mind about buying the plane at all if the true costs had been known when it was approved.

The Navy submarine rescue vehicle is an even worse example of cost overrun. Originally, the Navy estimated that twelve of these vessels would cost $36 million, or $3 million each. Later in the hearings that the Economy in Government Subcommittee held, we dug out the fact that the total cost would not be $36 million, but $460 million, and that, instead of twelve vessels, the number had been cut to six. The unit costs had escalated from $3 million to $77 million each. And the irony was that after examining the nature of submarine accidents it became apparent that the vehicle could have been crucial in only two operations since 1927.

A third example involves our most important strategic

missile. The Committee found that the costs of Minuteman II—and Minuteman III is yet to come—skyrocketed from $3 billion to $7 billion.

These are not unique or exceptional examples. Costs on almost all weapons greatly exceed their original estimates by far more than can be accounted for by routine changes or average inflation.

In his *Washington Monthly* article, Robert S. Benson, who had served in the DOD office of the Comptroller under former Secretary of Defense Robert S. McNamara, stated:

> Few Americans are aware that about 90 per cent of the major weapons systems that the Defense Department procures ends up costing at least twice as much as was originally estimated.

C. H. Danhof in *Government Contracting and Technological Change* (Washington, D.C.: The Brookings Institution, 1968) wrote:

> During the 1950's virtually all large military contracts reflected an acceptance by the military agencies of contractor estimates which proved highly optimistic. Such contracts ultimately involved costs in excess of original contractual estimates of from 300 to 700 per cent.

The low initial estimates when weapons systems are authorized are not a matter of minor misjudgment or good faith miscalculation. The disgraceful fact is that neither the contractors nor the Pentagon tells the truth about the cost of the weapons. They deliberately lie about the cost. They deceive Congress. They deceive the public. They purposely underestimate the cost of these weapons systems in order to get them established and to get Congress and the country committed to them.

What is most appalling is the uncritical way in which cost overruns and supply surpluses are accepted by the Pentagon. They treat a $2 billion overrun as if it were small change. To be consistently wrong on the estimates of cost, as the Pentagon has been, should bring the entire system of contracting under the most detailed scrutiny. But there is not the slightest indication that this is being done by the military itself. In fact, when such questions are raised, the services are far more defensively reluctant than eager to improve the system.

A military man, President Dwight D. Eisenhower, in his Farewell Address less than a decade ago, warned against the danger of "unwarranted influence, whether sought or unsought, by the military-industrial complex."

Today there exists, whether sought or unsought, that unwarranted influence. It results in excessive costs, burgeoning military budgets, and scandalous performances. The danger has long since materialized. It threatens our security. It has a ravaging effect on our nation's spending priorities, as it deflects us from the task of marshaling our funds and our civil organization to attack the pressing problems of our neglected cities, our polluted environment, our divided races, and our mistrustful young.

But to call what we live with today simply a "military-industrial complex" is to limit it incorrectly. What we face is a wider concentration of forces and influences. It is, in fact, a coalition of the military services, the service associations, the Pentagon bureaucracy, the giant aerospace industry, trade associations and public relations firms, the employees of the weapons makers and the trade unions that organize them, a vast proportion of the scientific and engineering talent in the country, universities whose departments have become dependent on Pentagon largesse, government-sponsored and privately owned research organizations, local business and civic groups whose communities grow and prosper on Pentagon contracts, and the local, state, and national politicians whose survival hinges on their active representation of these forces in their states or districts.

The complex has more tentacles than an octopus. Its dimen-

sions are almost infinite. It is a military–industrial–bureaucratic – trade-association – labor-union – intellectual – technical
–academic–service-club–political complex whose pervasiveness touches nearly every citizen.

It is necessary to detail some of its dimensions in order to
understand the real power of the Pentagon in our society.

To take an example, the Defense Department's entangle-
ment with academe is perhaps deeper than many Americans
off the campuses realize. In fiscal 1968, two great universities
were among the top 100 military contractors in the United
States. The Massachusetts Institute of Technology, with $125
million, ranked fifty-fourth, and Johns Hopkins University,
with $58 million, ranked eighty-fifth. In all, American edu-
cational and nonprofit institutions received more than $675
million in military prime contract awards. Of the top 500
defense contractors, ninety-nine were educational institutions.

The state of Massachusetts, with MIT and a bevy of nonprofit "think-tanks," got a third of all contracts going to educational institutions and 15 per cent of the Pentagon awards
to nonprofit institutions. There, the neo-academics who
work for the research organizations located along the Boston
bypass have the best of all worlds. By settling in Concord or
Lexington, they can pretend to be proper Bostonians, avoid
the problems of the inner city, and enjoy the luxury of living
on Pentagon subsidies. (Occasionally, they bite the hand that
feeds them by protesting the establishment of a local ABM
site when the reality of the work they do impinges too closely
on their personal lives.)

Almost half the DOD funds supporting nonprofit institutions went to California, which ranked third in funds going
to educational institutions. Enormous amounts were ear-
marked for Stanford University and for the Universities of
California at Berkeley, Los Angeles, La Jolla, and San
Diego—perhaps by way of proving how tolerant officialdom

can sometimes be, dispatching to the center of the military protest movement some $30 million a year in military subsidies.

The involvement of the universities in such research is not accidental. In 1967, the Defense Department initiated Project THEMIS to "stimulate the development of additional centers of defense-relevant research," and Dr. John Foster, who directs Pentagon research, told the Senate Foreign Relations Committee that THEMIS could provide "a wider geographical distribution of Defense research funds favoring institutions and areas which do not now receive substantial support." The Pentagon asked for $33 million for THEMIS in fiscal 1970. The funds would not only support 92 existing projects at 52 universities, but provide for 25 new projects as well. Projects are not limited to domestic American institutions; some 440 are carried out in 44 foreign countries, involving 62 foreign universities.

In the view of many thoughtful people, the Department of Defense is not the proper agency to run a federal aid-to-education program at home or abroad. Testifying before the Senate Armed Services Committee on the fiscal 1970 authorization for military procurement, Senator J. William Fulbright, of Arkansas, said:

> The increasing dependence of colleges and universities on the Defense Department largesse is not a healthy situation for the institutions, the students, or for our free society. The type of thinking that assumes a role for the Defense Department in subsidizing higher education, however, sees no conflict between the role of the academician as a teacher and independent thinker and as a hireling of the Defense Department.

But, despite such reservations, the military-industrial complex now includes very large numbers of students and employees of the colleges and universities, as well as many thousands of men and women who work on Pentagon-funded research projects in nonprofit corporations and private businesses.

The military-industrial complex also includes more than 3.4 million soldiers, sailors, Marines, and fliers, 1.3 million civilians who work directly for the Defense Department, and 100,000 companies that work on defense orders and employ 3.8 million civilians. About one out of six or seven families in the United States is dependent on the complex for a livelihood.

On the military side proper, the military-industrial complex includes 18 Army and 4 Marine Corps divisions, 5 Army regiments, 11 infantry brigades, 60 air defense artillery battalions, 7 Special Forces groups, an Army missile command, 10,465 planes in the Army's active aircraft inventory, 932 Navy ships including 423 warships and 17 carriers, 3 Marine air wings made up from the 8,491 planes of all kinds under Navy jurisdiction, 10 antisubmarine air groups, and 15,327 Air Force planes in 72 wings, of which 21 are strategic, 43 tactical, and 8 for air defense.

Additionally, there are the strategic forces upon which depends the safety of the nation against nuclear attack from the Soviet Union or Communist China. These are awesome forces, indeed, their purpose being, in the words of former Secretary of Defense Clark Clifford, to deter attack by "their ability, even after absorbing a well-coordinated surprise strike, to inflict unacceptable damage on the attacker." They include 1,054 land-based intercontinental ballistic missiles (ICBM's), most of which are Minuteman missiles, 41 Polaris submarines with 656 submarine-launched ballistic missiles, (SLBM's), 646 nuclear-armed strategic Air Force bombers, numerous medium-range missiles and bombers deployed on the periphery of the Soviet Union and China as deterrent forces, and, it is known from public sources, over 6,500 nuclear warheads.

The value of the property holdings of the Department of

Defense provides another measure of the mammoth economic power wielded by the military side of the complex.
DOD-owned land and buildings and long-life items like
ships, valued at their acquisition cost alone, are worth more
than $40 billion. At present prices, much of the land is many
times more valuable. Examples from among the hundreds of
sites spring easily to mind: Treasure Island in San Francisco
Bay and the land outside Atlanta, Georgia, purchased by the
Air Force years ago for $400 an acre, and now used by Lock-
heed Aircraft. The Department of Defense has become the
nation's largest landlord.

On top of this, the Pentagon's personal property inventory, valued at existing prices, is worth four times the
amount of its real property, or $162 billion. Included in this
total are almost $12 billion in plants and equipment that the
military owns outright and another $4 billion in material
provided to contractors. The grand total is $202.5 billion of
real and personal property in the hands of the military.

Equally revealing of the military side's pervasiveness are
the 429 major bases and 2,972 minor bases found scattered
over thirty countries throughout the world. Most of these
bases are leased, rather than owned outright, and do not
show up in the figure for property holdings. Physically, they
cover some 4,000 square miles. More than 1 million men and
500,000 of their dependents live on them; 250,000 foreign
employees work at them. Their annual cost to the United
States exceeds $4.5 billion—mechanical maintenance alone
comes to $660 million—and they drain $2.5 billion annually
from the U.S. balance of payments.

The facts and figures for the industrial side of the complex are as staggering. In 1969, the Pentagon spent $38.8
billion on military prime contracts of $10,000 or more. The
top 100 companies got $25.2 billion—that is, 68.2 per cent,
or over two-thirds, of the total. The top ten got $11 billion
in contracts—almost 30 per cent. The top five alone received

$7 billion in prime contracts—almost 20 per cent of all the prime contract awards. Because the prizes that go to defense industry are so lucrative, the forces deployed to influence where the money goes almost match in political megatonnage the military might of the weapons themselves. The huge stakes are fought over fiercely. "Who gets the gravy?" is the issue.

What firms get these contracts, where they are located, and the kinds of military hardware they make tell more about the military-industrial complex than anything else. The answers, in fact, tell what the military-industrial complex is all about.

During World War II, almost all the big weapons contractors were firms that had converted to war production at the onset of hostilities. When the fighting ended, most of them reconverted to peacetime production, switching back to plowshares, washing machines, refrigerators, automobiles, and sporting equipment.

In this age of highly complex weaponry, such conversion is no longer readily possible. Before World War II, ships, tanks, trucks, jeeps, rifles, machine guns, and artillery were the big hardware items. Now they make up only one-seventh of all military hard goods, while aircraft, missiles, and electronic and communications equipment are almost 70 per cent of the total. This change is perhaps the major reason for the unwarranted influence of the military-industrial complex. The big contractors are engaged almost solidly in military production and very little else.

The important names among the top military contractors in World War II were General Motors, Chrysler, Ford, U.S. Steel, Kaiser, General Electric, and a few aircraft firms. Today, nine of the top dozen are huge aerospace companies. They make the missiles, the radars, computers, and gyroscopes, and the supersonic planes. And they receive one-third of all prime military contracts. Then, military procurement was only a part of a company's total business. Now, military contracts dominate the business of nine of the top twelve companies.

In the 1960's, only three firms among the top dozen military contractors did less than 50 per cent of their work for the military. These were General Electric (19 per cent), American Telephone and Telegraph (9 per cent), and General Motors (2 per cent). Firms like Lockheed, General Dynamics, McDonnell Douglas, Ling-Temco-Vought, North American Rockwell, Grumman Aircraft, and Avco Corporation—all generally found in the top dozen every year—did over two-thirds of their business with the Pentagon. When space and atomic energy awards are added in, the concentration of these firms' business with the defense Establishment was even greater.

The fact is that most of the big military contractors could not survive without weapons business. They have their noses and both feet in the Pentagon procurement trough.

Where the fat defense contracts go is one of the more interesting aspects of the military-industrial complex. Almost 30 per cent of all prime military awards are to firms in California and Texas.

California led all the states in prime contracts received in eight major categories. It was first in contracts for missile and space systems (46 per cent of the national total), military building supplies (44 per cent), subsistence (23 per cent), electronics and communications equipment (21 per cent), construction (19.6 per cent), other aircraft equipment and supplies (19.5 per cent), weapons (15 per cent), and all other supplies and equipment (11.5 per cent). Texas led in the airframe and spare parts category (37 per cent), petroleum (33 per cent), and ammunition (11 per cent).

Five states alone got 82 per cent of the $6.1 billion spent for airframe contracts. Of the $2.5 billion spent on aircraft engine and related spares, 90 per cent was disbursed in only five states, and five states got 71 per cent of the $5 billion spent on missile and space systems. The reason for this concentration is that the contracts went to the big new aerospace industries: General Dynamics in Texas; Lockheed in Georgia; McDonnell Douglas in Missouri; North American Rockwell and Lockheed in California; and Boeing in Washington.

In the past, apologists for weapons contractors argued that such facts distorted the picture. Although no really good data were available, the apologists nonetheless asserted that, in practice, there was a much greater dispersal of contracts, because of the vast number of small subcontractors who performed work for the "primes." But an interesting study by C-E-I-R, Inc., entitled *Economic Impact Analysis of Subcontracting Procurement Patterns,* upset such reasoning. *Business Week* headlined an article describing the study as the "End of a Myth."

What the C-E-I-R report showed was that in defense work the main subcontractor for a prime contractor provided over a third of the value of all the subcontracting work. The top ten subcontractors for prime contractors accounted for 80 per cent or more of all the subcontracting effort. In addition, the leading subcontractors were often major prime contractors themselves. The study found that 18 of the 26 leading subcontractors were on the list of the 100 top defense contractors. Each got a piece of the business on some other company's weapons system contract.

As with the prime contractors, the heaviest concentration of subcontractors was in the missile and space industry. Here, 92 per cent of the value of all subcontracts was in the hands of only ten companies.

The concentration by states was even heavier for the subcontractors than for the prime contractors. As expected, California led the list. Eight of the top ten subcontractor states also appeared on the list of the top ten prime contractor states. But the ten leading subcontractor states had 75 per cent of all subcontracts while the ten top prime contractor states had only 67 per cent of the business.

The conclusion: defense subcontracts are even more concentrated than the prime contracts. Big companies merely change hats from prime to subcontractor, when going from one weapon system to another. The subcontractor on weapon system A becomes the prime contractor on weapon system B, while the prime contractor on weapon system B is a subcontractor on weapon system A.

Take, for example, the Sentinel-Safeguard anti-ballistic-missile system. The prime contractor on the ABM is Western Electric, AT&T's biggest military contractor subsidiary; it does almost 80 per cent of the defense work of AT&T, the nation's sixth largest contractor. The Martin Company, number 25 on the prime contractor list, subcontracts the Sprint missile. McDonnell Douglas, number 4, subcontracts to provide the Spartan missile elements of the system. The missile radar-site subcontractor is Raytheon, number 11 on the prime contractor list. General Electric, number 2 among the primes, is assigned the subcontract for the perimeter-acquisition radar component of the system. Sperry Rand's UNIVAC division, number 12, is charged with developing the data-processing subsystem.

The facts about defense subcontracting add to the evidence of massive concentration and mutual self-interest on the part of the major companies in the military-industrial complex and further explain why there is such a danger from the new munitions-makers and their opposite numbers in the Pentagon. With their high concentration of military business, the companies become dependent on military contracts. They have limited alternative business. There is no civilian market for their military goods. In business-page language, they are not sufficiently diversified. Even firms with less than half their work on military contracts may become dependent on these contracts because they provide the margin necessary to survival.

The Pentagon, in turn, becomes dependent on a very limited number of contractors. A concentration of technically sophisticated companies develops. The Pentagon needs them for the new weapons. They need the Pentagon to stay alive. Both are on a military-contract treadmill, characterized by initial cost underestimates, "buy-in" bidding, thousands of change orders, reduced specifications, "get-well" modifications, monumental cost overruns, imperfect weapons systems, little risk, and high profits. Many contracts are based on keeping the contractor busy rather than letting the harsh winds of price competition and quality performance carry the day. To keep the mutually dependent contractors in business, new weapons and improved models are constantly devised. Detroit's automobile design practices have been adapted to new weapons systems, which are characterized by built-in obsolescence, annual model changes, and excessive firepower.

The Pentagon justifies its excesses on the grounds that it must have an "in-place" industrial base, claiming that there is no way to convert quickly from cars and trucks to the black boxes and electronic brains of the new weapons systems. And why should it worry? In this marriage of convenience, there is no incentive to reduce costs or improve efficiency. A third party, the taxpayer, foots the bill.

Gordon Rule, a highly competent Navy civilian cost expert, told our Subcommittee on Economy in Government that defense contractors and the services know that proposed weapons systems will cost a great deal more than the original estimates or bids. Responding to questioning by one of our subcommittee members, Representative William S. Moorhead, Rule answered in straightforward language.

> Let me put it this way. I think that one of the things that we have got to stop doing in our contracting is playing games— the government and the contractor. We play games. We know that if we tell the DOD across the river how much something

is really going to cost, they may scrub it. And they know that if they tell the Congress how much it is really going to cost the Congress may scrub it.

So you start in with both sides knowing that it is going to cost more. . . . This is what we do. And this is ridiculous. And this is why we get into trouble. How you knock it off I don't know.

The testimony continued:

REPRESENTATIVE MOORHEAD. It is absolutely clear that they have been playing games with us—

MR. RULE. Of course.

REPRESENTATIVE MOORHEAD. If the Air Force wants a C-5A and they give us a price that is indeed what it will cost, they run a greater chance of having the program turned down.

MR. RULE. You might not get the program, that is right. So we start knowing that it is going to cost more, and we are so deep in down the road that we get more money. There is no question about this.

After further development of this point, I intervened. Speaking as the chairman of the Subcommittee, I said,

Mr. Rule, the statement you have just made to Congressman Moorhead, if the Pentagon were honest with the contractor and the contractor honest with the Pentagon, and the Pentagon honest with Congress, and Congress honest with itself, we might scrub some of these weapons systems, is one of the most revealing and significant statements that has been made in these whole hearings. It is an excellent statement.

"And we are being lied to?" I asked. "Is that what you are telling us?"

"That word 'lied' and that word 'honest' are your words, not mine." Rule answered, and went on, "I said we were playing games."

Whatever the words, obviously and, it seems to me, inevitably, defense contractors and the military services working on particular weapons systems develop a community of interest. Both want the new weapon. Both become champions and advocates of what they are trying to sell. When later, compounding the dangers of a faulty set-up, the service becomes auditor of the contract, it is like putting the fox in charge of the hen house.

Four times a year, the highest echelons of the DOD meet with their industrial counterparts, the twenty-one members of the Industry Advisory Council, to discuss mutual problems and chart the nation's defense future. With the presidents and chairmen of the big companies—Boeing, General Electric, IBM, Northrop, AVCO, General Dynamics, AT&T, Litton, and others—Pentagon officials discuss an agenda covering the major problems of the military-industrial complex at length during two-day conferences. Admiral Rickover told our Economy in Government Subcommittee:

> I believe that for most high level government officials the Industrial Advisory Council is their only real contact with the procurement world. As a result, their viewpoint is influenced by what they hear from industry executives during these meetings.

Similarly, the executives are influenced by what they hear. When the Pentagon determines to sell a new weapon system, all the stops are pulled out. Detailed briefings are made to the Industry Advisory Council.

Then, after the industrial allies have been briefed, the public relations experts are deployed to persuade others of the virtue of Pentagon plans. Some 200 civilian and military members of the staff of the Assistant Secretary of Defense for Public Affairs stand ready to provide "positive" information to the press, public, and Congress. This office's budget of $1.6 million a year pays the freight for experts on community relations, speakers to explain new weapons systems, briefings on a wide range of military issues, and ghost-written articles for submission to editors of both popular and technical publications.

In place for Pentagon use during legislative battles (like that over the ABM in the late summer of 1969), are a dazzling array of radio, television, film, poster, advertising, and exhibit resources. Also available for help are the legislative lobbies of the DOD and the three services. Their eighty professionals not only provide a great deal of necessary information and work on servicemen's cases for congressional offices, but are also at the beck and call of House and Senate members for briefings, data, and arrangements for inspection tours of military weapons and bases.

In addition to the DOD Public Affairs Office and the legislative lobby, the Secretary of Defense has at hand a $5.3 million annual budget for the Office of Information for the Armed Forces, which operates throughout the world and reaches both civilian and military audiences. Under it are the Armed Forces Radio and Television Service and the Armed Forces Motion Picture, Publications and Press Service. Together, they spend about $12 million a year on "information." The two services operate 350 radio and TV stations throughout the world. Yearly, they produce about 50 films, print 8.5 million copies of 70-odd publications, and distribute 400,000 copies of posters. They also provide articles and photos for some 1,500 newspapers run by the military.

Funds for the individual services more than rival those available to the DOD itself. The Army spends $2 million a year on its Office of Information to sustain and improve its "image" through appearances of the Army Field Band and operation of the Army Hometown News Center, the Army Exhibit Unit, and field offices in Los Angeles and New York. It spends an additional $4.9 million for Army-wide information and community relations activities. The Navy duplicates the Army's advertising efforts with a headquarters public affairs office in Washington and field branches in New York,

Chicago, and Los Angeles. It, too, provides news to local papers through the Fleet Hometown News Center, and it maintains the Navy-Marine Corps Exhibit Center. These activities set taxpayers back by $1.4 million a year, but that sum is small potatoes compared with the additional $9.9 million the Navy spends on other public information and community relations programs. Not to be overshadowed by their sister services, the Marine Corps and Air Force spend $2.7 and $9 million a year, respectively, on operating expenses and salaries for their public affairs operations.

All of this adds up to a whopping $47.3 million a year for military public relations.

When the fight over the ABM system was first joined, General Alfred D. Starbird, manager of the Sentinel-Safeguard project, ordered the Army's Chief of Information to deploy all of his public relations weapons in pursuit of a legislative victory. A seventeen-page memo from the General commanded that "magazine articles will be prepared by Army staff members . . . for submission to military, scientific, and professional journals and publications that are service sponsored or oriented."

In his master plan for a "public relations public affairs program on a country-wide basis," the General also called on his subordinates to "encourage and assist in the preparation of magazine articles . . . by civilian scientific or technical writers of national stature." Speaking engagements were arranged. A public affairs coordinating committee was ordered established. Information kits, press releases, film clips, slides, and exhibits were readied. Pentagon briefings were set up. One group trekked off to the AFL-CIO headquarters just north of the White House where they briefed members of the Construction Trades Council and the Industrial Union Department on the construction manpower requirements for the ABM system. Three- and four-page reports of the briefing, along with Army photos and sketches on how the ABM worked, shortly appeared in the monthly publication of some of the country's largest unions.

Had all of the promotion plans of the Starbird memo been put into effect, very little of the vast $30 million strategic public relations resources of the Pentagon would have been held in reserve. But the Pentagon's first-strike public relations capacity was foiled when an enterprising reporter published details of the General's memo and the nationwide campaign to sell ABM like soup was officially called off.

When I inquired about the Starbird campaign effort, the acting Assistant Secretary of Defense for Public Affairs, Daniel Z. Henkin, wrote to me on July 28, 1969:

> In regard to your inquiry concerning funds spent by the Department of Defense on promotional activities on behalf of the Sentinel and Safeguard ABM proposals, no funds of the Office of the Secretary of Defense were or have been allocated for "promotional activities" related to either of these proposals.

Possibly no funds were specifically "allocated" or charged against an ABM account for promotional activities for ABM, but it was certainly obvious that hundreds of Pentagon man-hours and millions in resources were spent promoting the system.

Publication of the Starbird internal memorandum had a salutary effect in that it did stop the official propaganda effort. But it could not stop one aspect of the plan ordering those associated with the program to "cooperate and coordinate with industry on public relations efforts by industries involved in the Sentinel program."

One of the weapons fired in the battle when the ABM issue was before the Senate, with an initial $10 to $12 billion at stake, was an Opinion Research Corporation Poll ostensibly proving that "84 per cent of all Americans support an ABM system." Immediately, an organization called the Citizens

Committee for Peace with Security took advertising space in twenty-five major newspapers throughout the country to proclaim this astonishing support.

Shortly afterward, it was revealed that 55 per cent of the signers of the advertisement had defense-industry connections. Fourteen were directors, officers, or lawyers of companies that had received portions of the $1 billion already spent on research-and-development activities for the system. Another twenty were connected with firms who were listed among the top 100 military contractors. Twenty-one others were connected with ABM subcontractors or smaller military contractors not in the top 100 category. At this point, Opinion Research repudiated the poll and claimed that the ABM advocates had distorted the results.

This frustration of the Pentagon's armada of public relations weapons was the result of the Senate's review of the ABM—the first major critical public review of any weapon system since the end of World War II. It was a beginning. But more must be done.

I believe that as citizens, as officials, as servicemen, as American taxpayers, we must look hard at all of the consequences of our uncritical attitude toward the Pentagon. We must examine in detail the overruns, inefficiencies, and aborted weapons systems the military-industrial complex has spawned. We must calculate closely what the wastefulness and power of the Pentagon costs us.

Those of us who serve in Congress have a special responsibility.

We must study and recommend means whereby the military budget can be reduced without sacrificing the safety or security of the United States. We must spell out the way the system rewards those high-ranking military and civilian officials who cooperate with it, not neglecting to describe the role that Congress itself has played in building up the unwarranted influence the military-industrial complex now exercises.

Finally, we, who have heard their testimony, must speak out about the way the monster we have allowed to grow punishes those who criticize its customs.

There have been a few such brave men.

II

Patriots in Trouble

UNTIL LATE 1968, John McGee and A. Ernest Fitzgerald had never heard of each other. But they had much in common. McGee was a Navy fuel inspector in Thailand. He uncovered large-scale corruption. Instead of rewarding him, the Navy tried to fire him. Fitzgerald was a high-level civilian cost-analyst in the office of the Secretary of the Air Force. He revealed the galloping waste of U.S. taxpayers' money on the big weapons systems—the C-5A Galaxy cargo plane, the Minuteman missiles, and the Mark II radar and computer brain for the F-111 fighter plane. Like its sister service, instead of promoting the man who blew the whistle, the Air Force first assigned Fitzgerald to a meaningless job and, later, through a "reduction in force," got rid of him altogether.

Both men had come to the government as highly qualified specialists. McGee had worked for oil companies in the field before he signed on with the Navy. Fitzgerald was an efficiency expert with experience in private industry before the Air Force hired him; in fact, before he spotted the huge cost overruns on the C-5A airplane at Lockheed Aircraft's factory, he had been in the plant as a civilian cost expert.

The two men were to end up with one other thing in common: a small country in Asia. The Navy sent McGee home when he complained about the theft of 5.5 million gallons of fuel in Thailand. Ernie Fitzgerald, removed from his duties analyzing costs of weapons systems, was told to look into the cost of a bowling alley the Air Force was building in Thailand.

The moral of both stories is simple. If you do your duty, uncover waste and corruption, and perform a public service, the military bureaucracy will attack you instead of the waste or corruption. You will be reassigned, your responsibilities curtailed.

What happened to these two men demonstrates how the system under which the military-industrial complex operates promotes waste and penalizes efficiency.

John McGee, born in Mississippi in 1933, joined the Navy during the Korean War and served on the destroyer tender *Shenandoah* and the destroyer *Willard Keith*. Diligent and energetic, he took correspondence courses from the Armed Forces Institute and earned a college completion certificate. After his discharge, his first job was as a laboratory technician with one of the giant oil and natural gas producers in New Mexico. Then he worked for a petroleum engineering firm in Texas and moved on to Wyoming to become the petroleum engineer in charge of a five-state office. Because the exploration and engineering work in the field was a relatively unstable business, McGee went to work as a civilian fuel inspector for the Navy in 1966. The understanding was that after a short tour in Vietnam he would receive a permanent position in Thailand as a replacement for the only civilian fuel inspector there on behalf of the U.S. Defense Department.

On his way to Vietnam, McGee stopped off for a 10-day orientation period in Thailand. His time was spent not on the job, as he had assumed it would be, but in bowling, golfing, wining, and dining. All this was provided by the man he was to have replaced but who, McGee found on his return, was kept on as his superior.

McGee's suspicions were aroused. The first thing he noticed on his return to Thailand from Vietnam was that his superior was signing receipts for oil on behalf of receiving activities many miles away and for which he had no invoices or evidence of any kind that the oil had actually been received. These documents were the basis for payments to the big oil firms who were picking up the tab for the kind of wining and dining McGee had been treated to ten months earlier, and for weekends at the company resort cottages. When McGee raised questions about the procedures for receipting deliveries, his colleague threatened to remove him if he complained. When he asked one of the oil companies for supporting documents, he was banished to the oil terminal on the outskirts of Bangkok, where, isolated from the contracts and documents at the main office, he became an inspector unable to inspect.

Informally, in June, 1967, and again through established grievance procedures, McGee protested and made allegations regarding the deficiencies he had observed. He was told that the issues he raised were irrelevant. Finally, in March, 1968, John McGee wrote to me alleging that there were serious deficiencies in the procedures for the delivery and receipt of fuel—petroleum, oils, and lubricants—to American military installations in Thailand. He said that shortages, thefts, and serious improprieties had resulted.

After determining that he was serious in his allegations

and that he had independent evidence to support them, I asked the General Accounting Office (GAO) to investigate the charges. In a report made to me in January, 1969, the General Accounting Office supported McGee's allegations—the same allegations he had repeatedly tried to make through official channels, only to have them stifled by his immediate superior as well as by the head of the U.S. Navy Fuel Supply Office in Alexandria, Virginia.

The GAO report stated:

> The control system for distribution of POL [petroleum, oils, and lubricants] and the processing of Government documents for POL payments were deficient and did not adequately protect the interest of the Government.

With respect to verifying the delivery of fuel supplied to vehicles under service-station contracts, one of the three main methods of distributing fuel in Thailand, the GAO added that it found no evidence that verification of fuel deliveries had been made between January and October, 1967—the period of time that it audited—and that, as McGee had alleged:

> The Sub-Area Petroleum Office in Thailand and the Inspector of Petroleum in Bangkok did not receive independent and documented verifications of the receipt of fuel supplies from the receiving bases prior to signing the Orders for Supplies or Services.

The report also said:

> The responsible officers acted imprudently in not obtaining documented verifications from the receiving activities that the fuel shown on the contractors' delivery documents had actually been received.

The General Accounting Office found that, for the period of its audit alone, at least 5.5 million gallons of fuel were stolen or unaccounted for. For example, of the 1,128,700 gallons allegedly delivered under service-station contracts, over 52 per cent was either stolen or not received and, of 7.4 million gallons of diesel fuel said to be delivered in 1967 to the Udorn Air Force Base in Thailand, some 3 million gallons (40 per cent) were not received. The military itself acknowledged that an additional 2 million gallons of fuel had been delivered but not received during 1967. The total amount included some 371,000 gallons delivered to a fictitious unit named "COMM. U.S. Air Force," 220,000 gallons of fuel stolen under service-station contracts, 378 truckloads of fuel totaling over 1.2 million gallons wholly or partially stolen, and 338 truckloads of J-4 jet fuel stolen or not delivered at various times from April, 1967, through June, 1968. The GAO investigation, which merely sampled some deliveries in a representative period, clearly indicated the alarming extent of corruption in American military operations in Thailand during this period—corruption that, but for McGee, might never have been exposed.

But, unhappily, as so often happens, responsible officers attacked the man who had told instead of attacking the problem he had laid bare. McGee was reprimanded. He was denied a routine, in-grade pay increase—a step that is ordinarily automatic. Official attempts were made to remove him from his post by the commanding officer, U.S. Navy Fuel Supply Center. Other steps to fire him were proposed.

In January, 1969, I asked the Secretary of the Navy to make an independent review of the case, for I believed that McGee was the subject of punitive action because of his courageous revelations.

The Secretary, Paul R. Ignatius, in turn asked the Civil Service Commission to make an impartial investigation of the personnel actions against McGee. This the Commission did, finding that, through negligence and imprudent actions, McGee's superiors had contributed to the conditions that had made possible the thefts of petroleum in Thailand. Yet, when McGee successfully exposed the system that had invited corruption, the Navy called "foot faults" on him. Its zeal in digging up irrelevant details of his past was matched only by its failure to change the lax inspection system.

On April 18, 1969, the new Secretary of the Navy, John Chaffee, made a decision with respect to McGee and released a statement concerning it. The Navy withdrew its reprimand. McGee was also granted the long overdue routine ingrade pay increase. However, the Navy's action in removing the reprimand and in granting the belated step increase was grudging and backhanded, and, in certain respects, what the service had to say at this time was clearly wrong.

I had urged that McGee be commended, not reprimanded. The Navy said that they found no basis for commending him "insomuch as the disclosure of improper fuel operations was not initiated by Mr. McGee but had been reported earlier by others." In that statement, the Navy was setting up a straw man to bowl over. Let me explain why.

Some isolated cases of theft in Thailand were known, and some minor actions against specific individuals had been taken at the time McGee arrived in Thailand in May, 1967. But what McGee spotted almost immediately was a system whereby the only fuel inspector in Thailand certified the receipt of hundreds of thousands of gallons of fuel on the basis of documents that he did not check out or verify. What McGee alleged was that this system made it possible for the thefts and the wrongdoing both to exist and to continue. No one had disclosed anything of this order earlier.

McGee was proven correct by the GAO report confirming his charges, which also confirmed that the massive thefts continued to take place for months after he had first raised this fundamental issue. Not until September, 1968, fifteen months after McGee first brought the problem to the attention of his superiors, were changes made in the procedure with respect to ground fuels, which was one of the three major categories of fuels delivered in Thailand. In other words, without McGee's actions, the GAO investigation and report would not have been made, and, except for his action and the GAO report, the basic system would no doubt still continue to be used—a system that the GAO called both deficient and imprudent, and said failed to protect the interests of the United States of America.

The Navy release also claimed that extensive study of the matter "revealed no evidence to support McGee's charges that his supervisor had fraudulently receipted for fuel deliveries in Thailand." That this statement is wrong I can assert without qualification. Let us look at the facts.

John McGee alleged only that his supervisor had certified that many fraudulent receipts were correct. McGee did not allege that the supervisor himself had signed the original fraudulent receipts. What happened was this. Fuel was shipped out from Bangkok to bases or stations all over Thailand. As the GAO found out, hundreds of truckloads were never delivered. Sometimes, receipts were made out for fictitious bases. At times, false names were used; at other times, the receipts were illegible.

McGee's supervisor was in Bangkok. Without ever seeing the receipts for deliveries of hundreds of truckloads and millions of gallons of fuel, this man signed a statement on Form DD 250 that he had confirmed the shipment information with the receiving activity and that he was signing for the receipt of the fuel on their behalf.

I have one such form in my possession. It covers hundreds of shipments totaling 2,548,680 gallons of jet fuel, grade JP4. The cost for this grade of kerosene is given as $230,553.59. Attached to this form are twenty-three pages giving the facts about each shipment. This includes the dates when the fuel was shipped and received, the number of trucks delivering the fuel, and the receipt numbers for the shipments.

Without checking them out, McGee's supervisor certified that such receipts were accurate, that the fuel had been delivered, and that the contractors should be paid. On this basis, the contractors were paid for deliveries, some of which were never made to U.S. bases. It was this practice on the part of his supervisor to which McGee properly objected.

When the Navy canceled its pending letter of reprimand against McGee, a letter charging him with "alleged falsification on an employment application," it gave two reasons for the cancellation. One was procedural errors in prosecuting disciplinary action against McGee. The second was its own failure to move promptly or properly in other respects.

But the wording of the Navy's cancellation leads one to think that only procedural errors and delays had led to withdrawal of the reprimand. In effect, the Navy let stand its punitive charge against McGee—namely, that he falsified an employment application—even while withdrawing the reprimand based on that false charge.

This employment application charge was important to McGee, and the point needs explanation. On August 16, 1968, the commanding officer of the U.S. Navy Fuel Supply Office gave McGee a "notice of proposed removal" from his job in Bangkok. Under the specifications, the notice charged that McGee's standard Form 57, which he submitted when he was hired in April, 1966, contained "false information." It was said that he concealed the fact that he had been previously employed by the Air Force, in the period 1955–56. Yet on the first page of that Form 57, McGee specifically listed his employment in 1955 and 1956. Far from concealing this matter, he listed it on the very form on which the Navy charged that he had concealed it.

In addition, when he was interviewed, the point of his previous employment had been brought up and discussed, and it had an important bearing on his new status. When he went to work for the Navy in 1966, he was not being hired as a government employee for the first time; he was officially "reinstated." His official forms—those forms that every employee receives when any personnel action is taken about him—indicated that his employment was a "reinstatement." Finally, McGee has a letter dated April, 1966, from the Civil Service Commission signed by John Macy, Jr., then the Chairman, referring to his "reinstatement."

I have a copy of the letter from Chairman Macy. It reads in part:

> The records show that on the basis of your former Federal employment and your veterans preference you have unlimited time eligibility for reinstatement to any position in the competitive service for which you can meet the requirements.

I also have a copy of a letter sent to McGee by the recruiting representative, Harry N. Ogilvie, dated April 29, 1969. Remember that McGee was charged with concealing his prior employment when submitting his Form 57 application for employment. Yet Ogilvie wrote to McGee before he was reemployed:

> We received your SF 57 from Cdr. Tinney today.
> Upon review, I noted that you indicate that you were previously employed by the Federal Government as a GS-4 Clerk, Security Patrol.

McGee was not reprimanded. Nor was he fired. He was not to go unpunished, however. He was ordered to Pensacola, Florida, as a laboratory technician to test oil samples—a job he had done many years before, early in his career.

What the Navy said loud and clear in the McGee case was: To get along, go along. Don't report any wrongdoing. If methods are lax, if officials are imprudent, if no one will act, do not do anything about it. If you do, you may well be reprimanded. Instead of investigating the problem, we will investigate you. Your life for the past decade will be examined in full detail. Your old forms will be scrutinized for any minor error. You can expect no automatic in-grade pay increases or promotions. In fact, we will try to fire you. Instead of being commended for a job well done, you will be looked upon as a maverick and ostracized by the system.

That, I am sorry to say, is the real meaning of the case of John McGee. And that, too, is the meaning of the case of A. E. Fitzgerald.

In a line from a now famous memorandum he wrote to Air Force General J. W. O'Neill on the huge cost overruns in the Minuteman missile program, Ernie Fitzgerald tells a great deal about himself. "The solution to this problem," he said, "is ultra simple: Tell the truth, no matter how painful."

The statement essentially characterizes the man. But Fitzgerald, despite his serious demeanor and determined countenance, is not overwhelmed by a sense of self-righteousness. At his first appearance before the Subcommittee on Economy in Government, in November, 1968, he revealed the $2 billion cost overrun of the C-5A airplane. In June, 1969, testifying again, he revealed that he had been relieved of his major responsibilities and was no longer involved in the cost analysis for the major weapons systems. The following colloquy took place between Fitzgerald and Senator Len B. Jordan of Idaho, the Subcommittee's ranking minority member.

SENATOR JORDAN. "What duties were given to you in lieu of these previous duties which occupied 90 to 95 per cent of your time? You weren't left sitting idly there, were you?"

MR. FITZGERALD. "No, sir, not at all. I think that anyone at any responsible level in the Pentagon who is idle is idle because he wants to be. I have not been idle at all. I have had some unusual assignments which haven't really developed yet, which I presume took the place of these. One was to review the minor construction problems in Thailand. And the other was—"

SENATOR JORDAN. "Of what nature were these construction problems in Thailand?"

MR. FITZGERALD. "The principal one that was brought to my attention was the cost increase on the construction of a 20-lane bowling alley." (laughter).

"I don't mean to make light of that, it is a very important thing, and someone must do it," Fitzgerald added, tongue in cheek.

"The other item that has been added, which I have not yet gotten into at all, is the problem of food service cost, that is, high cost in our mess halls." (laughter).

SENATOR JORDAN. "That is an important item too, is it not, of comparable weight with the bowling alley assignment?"

MR. FITZGERALD. "Yes, sir, approximately." (laughter).

Our Subcommittee had first heard of Ernest Fitzgerald, Deputy for Management Systems, Office of the Assistant Secretary of the Air Force, when we were searching for expert witnesses to testify during a three-day probe into procurement, profitability, and cost controls in the Pentagon's buying practices. Everyone spoke well of him. He was said to be tough and knowledgeable. We first invited him to testify on Wednesday, November 13, 1968.

The hearings took place in the oppressively appointed hearing room of the Senate Appropriations Committee in the New Senate Office Building. The meeting was called to order at 10:45 A.M. and Fitzgerald was asked to make a statement. To the surprise of the Subcommittee, he began by saying, "I do not have a prepared statement. I will have to speak extemporaneously this morning."

At that time, we knew that the cost for the 120 C-5A cargo planes and their spare parts had grown from $3.37 to $5.33 billion. We also knew, from a Pentagon staff briefing, that the Air Force knew it, too. They had known it the previous March when they had failed to reveal the overrun, even under questioning before the House Appropriations Commit-

tee. We knew that Fitzgerald knew all of this and we hoped
he would testify to the size of the overrun at our hearings.
But he was an official with the Air Force. It was more than
possible that he would hedge, qualify his remarks, or so dis-
semble that the facts would remain unclear. That is the way
most bureaucratic witnesses testify. At other times, they are
muzzled and carry out their orders. I forced the issue.

"Mr. Fitzgerald," I said, "I wrote you on October 18, and
asked that you prepare a statement in advance, and that you
submit 100 copies of your statement at least one day before
your appearance. You have told us this morning you did not
prepare a statement for the record. Why not?"

"Mr. Chairman," he replied, "I was directed not to prepare a statement."

"Who told you not to prepare the statement?" I asked.

"Directly my immediate superior," he said. But, he continued, his superior was in turn " . . . acting on the direction
of our legislative liaison people."

I then called the Pentagon's representative, Commander
Edward G. Dauchess, forward.

"So far as you know," I asked him, "is Mr. Fitzgerald free
to discuss issues before this committee if we ask him questions; provided of course, the questions do not deal with any
classified information?"

"Definitely," the Commander replied.

"He is free to answer?" I asked.

"Yes, sir," Commander Dauchess said.

I then asked Fitzgerald if it were true that the costs of the
C-5A under the contract they had with Lockheed Aircraft
and General Electric would be approximately $2 billion
more than originally estimated and agreed upon.

For the first time in any official response, Fitzgerald confirmed that fact. Furthermore, but not until after considerable difficulty with the Air Force, he provided detailed

proof for the record. Faced with the choice of telling the truth or obscuring it, he chose to be honest.

Fitzgerald's testimony on that early winter day captured the nation's attention. More than anything else, it triggered the now widespread and serious public concern over excessive costs and military waste. But Air Force reactions, far from easing public concern, merely served to heighten it. Things began to happen to Ernest Fitzgerald.

Two months before that November 13, Fitzgerald had been notified officially that his position with the Air Force was permanent. After three years on the job, he had what the Civil Service calls "career status." Twelve days after he testified, he lost his newly won tenure. The Air Force claimed that his status had been mistakenly conferred on him by "computer error." The coincidence of a misprogramed computer's just happening to make such a mistake in the case of a Pentagon official with the guts to tell a congressional committee that the Pentagon was spending too much was about as likely as the Joint Chiefs of Staff pleading for a big cut in the military budget.

Next, Fitzgerald was isolated from his old duties. No longer was he invited to the conferences to discuss the problems connected with the Minuteman missile, the Galaxy aircraft, and the Mark II electronic brain. Memoranda of meetings and cost tables were no longer distributed to him. Old friends at the Pentagon suddenly hardly knew him.

Meantime, his superiors were claiming with great vigor that he had not been penalized for his testimony. One of the strongest protests came from Secretary of the Air Force Harold Brown. On January 9, 1969, he said he was "shocked" at my statements objecting to the treatment of Fitzgerald. He insisted again that there had been only an "unfortunate error" in a newly installed computer program. He said Fitzgerald had "not been denied his rights, nor will he be in the future." Furthermore, the Secretary wrote to me, "he has not been penalized for testifying before your Committee by loss of career status."

At our next hearing on January 16, 1969, the truth came out.

I invited Secretary Brown to appear before the Subcommittee on Economy in Government to clear up this matter of Fitzgerald's status. He sent, instead, Assistant Secretary of the Air Force Robert Charles, who had devised the controversial C-5A contract. With him was Secretary Brown's chief personnel administrator, Thomas W. Nelson.

Under my questioning, Nelson testified that, in the eighteen months the computer had been in operation, there had been more than 16,000 personnel actions. Each time a change is made in the pay, grade, or status of an employee, the computer grinds out a page indicating the action taken. Copies are sent to the employee, the Civil Service, and other places. Since beginning operation, the computer had made only eight mistakes. Of these, only two had gone against the employee. The error in the Fitzgerald case was the only one ever made concerning the career status of any employee. The odds against it happening were at least one in 16,000.

I also questioned Assistant Secretary Charles. When I complained about the action taken against Fitzgerald, he replied, "I know of no action taken against him.

"Mr. Chairman, no one regrets more than I the coincidence that did occur."

Then I asked him if he knew whether any further action was planned or contemplated against Fitzgerald, and he answered; "I not only know of no further action that is planned against him, I know of none that has been taken against him."

Frankly, I didn't believe it. I had reason not to believe it. A copy of a memorandum, written to the Secretary, by Secretary Brown's administrative assistant, John A. Lang, Jr., had been sent to my office. It was dated January 6, 1969—two days before Secretary Brown had complained in his strongly worded letter to me that he was shocked that I would allege that Fitzgerald had been treated unfairly—and it proposed three ways "which could result in Mr. Fitzgerald's departure."

The first of these was "adverse actions—discharge, furlough, suspension, reduction in rank." The second was a "reduction in force." The memo also listed the rights involved "should charges be preferred or should his position be abolished."

It then went on to say, "There is a third possibility, which could result in Mr. Fitzgerald's departure." But, the memo continued, "This action is not recommended since it is rather underhanded and would probably not be approved by the Civil Service Commission."

I read this memo to Assistant Secretary Charles, who was testifying.

"It does not sound like an invitation to dismissal to me," he said.

I replied that if I were working for anyone and a memorandum like that were written about me, I would not consider that my employer was proposing a promotion.

The Assistant Secretary acknowledged that "the wording was unfortunate."

Of course, the memo directly contradicted the statements by Secretary Brown, by Charles himself, and by the personnel officer brought along to the hearing to explain matters. The truth was self-evident. As a result of Fitzgerald's testimony, the Air Force had not only denied him career status; it had detailed three possible ways to fire him. This was retaliation with a vengeance—the worst example I have seen in twelve years in the Senate.

And for what? What did Fitzgerald do? He told the truth. He gave Congress the facts. He acted in the public interest.

When Secretary Charles had finished his testimony, I called on Fitzgerald to testify again—and a new Air Force attempt at suppression of the facts was revealed.

At his previous appearance on November 13, Fitzgerald was asked by our Subcommittee to submit a number of documents for the record. These were so long in coming that their delay held up the printing of the hearings. Repeated requests were made to the Air Force for them. The key item we had requested was the Air Force's estimate of the C-5A overrun. When Fitzgerald first confirmed that the overrun was $2 billion, he was not putting forward his personal estimate and analysis. He was telling us what the Air Force's own estimate was—in a document that he and others knew about and had seen. Other documents we had asked for included proposals for "weighted guidelines" and a "lessons learned" paper by Fitzgerald's cost-cutting associate, Gordon Rule. Not until Christmas Eve had we received a package from the Air Force labeled "Inserts for the Record of Testimony of A. E. Fitzgerald."

One of my first questions to Fitzgerald was about these inserts.

He responded, "I was quite surprised that the submission had been forwarded without contacting me. I was not even aware that they had been forwarded."

Fitzgerald then testified that after he had had a chance to look at the inserts it was clear that the two documents he had promised to send had been omitted. Worse, the Air Force's estimate of a $2 billion cost overrun had been changed. The Air Force had substituted a much lower cost estimate of the C-5A overrun and tried to pass it off as a part of Fitzgerald's submission.

Unbelievable? It happened—like the "computer error" and the three-point memo on means of facilitating Fitzgerald's departure from the Air Force.

Our initial set of hearings attracted national attention. In

May, the Subcommittee issued a unanimous interim report of its findings and recommendations. Meanwhile, Fitzgerald and Gordon Rule appeared before a House subcommittee on which Congressman William S. Moorhead, of Pennsylvania, a member of our Committee, served. Facts on new cost over-runs were revealed. The Pentagon's attempts to protect Lockheed's stock came out. The Air Force scurried to order the second batch of the C-5A airplanes which, through a complicated process, would let the company recoup its costs on the first batch of the C-5A's.

In June, 1969, our Subcommittee on Economy in Government held a new set of hearings called for in the annual report of the full Joint Economic Committee and entitled "Hearings on the Military Budget and National Economic Priorities." In them, we deliberately sought witnesses whose views spanned the spectrum of responsible American political thought. They ranged from conservative Senator Barry Goldwater to liberal Professor John Kenneth Galbraith and from dovish Senator J. William Fulbright to hawkish former Secretary of State Dean Acheson.

On June 11, we probed again into military procurement. We heard from Barry Shillito, the Assistant Secretary of Defense for Installations and Logistics, and then called back Fitzgerald.

Fitzgerald's testimony was at odds with that of Assistant Secretary Shillito, who used all the proper words, but conveyed no sense of urgency. Vital matters were "under study" or "under constant review." The Defense Department was always "concerned" about this, that, or the other. In some areas, subjects were under "critical examination." In other areas, they were under "careful scrutiny."

After both men had finished, I said to Fitzgerald, "It is as if you were talking about two entirely different countries or departments of defense."

Fitzgerald's testimony was not as sensational as at his previous appearances. But he did bring out some very important information.

One of the excuses the Air Force was making for the huge cost increase on the C-5A was that it was caused in large part by inflation. The figure that Air Force spokesmen used was $500 million. Fitzgerald testified, however, that before the controversy became public, official Air Force estimates in documents he had seen put the figure at only $204 million.

He confirmed that costs on the Minuteman II missile had increased from $3 to over $7 billion—more than a 100 per cent rise.

He testified that Defense Secretary Robert S. McNamara was fed false information by the Air Force in the fall of 1967 about the cost of the C-5A airplane, and that the DOD Comptroller cautioned the Secretary that the amount would be much greater than the Air Force Chief of Staff had estimated. Fitzgerald also said he knew of twenty to thirty plants in which the U.S. government was knowingly allowing the contractors to charge higher prices in order to keep the plant open and the personnel employed. (This is called "providing for an assured capability.") He reported that shortly after one of his associates—an Air Force officer—questioned the cost of the C-5A, he ". . . was found to have unique qualifications to be the air attache in Addis Ababa."

When the questions to Fitzgerald were finished, I said to him: "You are a most unusual witness. You did more in alerting the Congress and the country on the problems of excessive waste in the military and overruns by your testimony before this Committee last November than anyone has done. In this connection, because of your experience and because of your ability, I wish you would return before this Committee on Friday morning."

I asked him to produce the estimates on the increase in the cost of the SRAM missile, which we had heard had gone up from $300 to $600 million in the past year. I asked for information concerning the Mark II avionics program—the radar and computer brain for the F-111 fighter plane. Specifically, I asked him for a Mark II "should-cost" study, which we knew existed. Finally, I asked him to produce information and memoranda on the attitudes towards costs and the way in which the pursuit of social goals was used as an excuse for inefficiency and cost increases in military contracts.

We eagerly awaited his return.

It was Friday, the 13th of June. The hearings were being covered by the television networks and the major newspapers in the country.

I opened the day's proceedings with a statement announcing that the chief executives of five of the biggest defense contractors had refused to appear at our hearings. The heads of Lockheed Aircraft, Boeing, General Dynamics, North American Rockwell, and Litton Industries had refused to appear. I said that their refusal to appear was surely the "new isolationism"—an obvious reference to the term President Richard Nixon had used against those of us who were questioning military spending when he had spoken at the Air Force Academy only a few days before.

How, in all good conscience, I asked, can these men who are so intimately involved in decisions that affect our national security and our $80 billion military outlays be so sanctimonious and uncooperative? I charged that their unresponsiveness heightened my suspicions concerning mismanagement and loose handling of the public trust.

I pointed out that these firms are sheltered from competition by negotiated and sole-source contracts and that among them are some who operate in plants built by the government, who use government-owned machinery, whose working capital is provided through progress payments, and whose profits are guaranteed through change orders, escalation clauses, and "sweetheart" options. I charged that most of them could not exist except for the huge noncompetitive Government contracts they receive and the special features and favors attending those contracts. They are sheltered from the harsh winds of free enterprise and competition by huge subsidies.

Waste weakens us, I said. Huge cost overruns destroy public confidence. I said it was the patriotic duty of the heads of these companies to appear voluntarily and to help us strengthen the fabric of our country and of our society.

Noting that we had provided an opportunity for all pertinent viewpoints to be reflected in the record, I said that we had had before us hawks and doves, Pentagon officials, budget officers, economists, efficiency analysts, and foreign policy experts. We believed that dialogue and debate and the conflict of opinion through adversary proceedings comprise the best way to find the truth. Indeed, I said, we had almost boxed the compass except for the views of one very important group—the big defense firms. We wanted to hear the contractor's side of it. We did not ask them to open their books or bring their records. We did not accuse them of any illegality. What we asked for was an explanation. In the past, I said, committees of Congress have often been charged with refusing to allow those who have been publicly criticized to have their day in the sun. We wanted to be fair and to do what was right. But the big defense contractors had turned us down. They apparently did not have enough confidence in their case to express it, argue it, and debate it. The failure to appear was strictly on their heads.

After I had delivered these strongly felt remarks, we then proceeded to hear from the Comptroller General of the United States, Elmer Staats. It was not until noon that Fitzgerald was called on to testify. By this time, the reporters and film crews had their stories. Some had left. Many were inattentive. It was everybody's judgment, including mine, that most of what we had asked Fitzgerald for was already public knowledge. We merely wanted him to document the facts for the record.

But news was about to break. The Pentagon had made a remarkable blunder. Just before the hearings began, at 10:00 A.M., a memorandum was delivered to Fitzgerald. Signed by his immediate superior, Assistant Secretary for Financial Management Thomas Nielsen of the Air Force, it gagged the witness. It refused to let him testify about any of the overruns on any of the weapons systems I had asked him to return to document—the C-5A, the Minuteman missile, the SRAM, and the Mark II avionics for the F-111 airplane. It did so on the grounds that Assistant Secretary Shillito had earlier agreed to provide this information to the Committee. The memorandum to Fitzgerald specifically stated:

> In view of the efforts underway by OSD (Office of the Secretary of Defense) to respond to Senator Proxmire's request, I believe it would be inappropriate for anyone from this office to release additional information concerning the programs mentioned in Senator Proxmire's letter of May 14, 1969, especially in open hearings.

That was a blockbuster. The information should be a matter of public record. It was not secret. It could not help a potential enemy. The Air Force had already postponed sending the information I asked for; it was to have been sent in a month, but on June 11th, we were told it would be another month or six weeks, although what I had asked for was known and available.

Wrong as the Pentagon's action was, it was also stupid. Much of what Fitzgerald might have said that day had been said before. The big news was the refusal of the five company presidents to appear before the Committee. At best, Fitzgerald's testimony might have been printed at the end of a long column of other information. When he finally appeared again four days later, what he said was given a prominence that it would never have received earlier.

For years, we had been hitting away at military waste. But it took the blunders of the Pentagon in the case of A. Ernest Fitzgerald to make these issues clear to the public.

If it were not for the loss to the country of the valuable services of a talented public servant in an area of critical importance, one might venture that this was the best thing that could have happened.

But on November 5, 1969, the Air Force eliminated Fitzgerald's position as Deputy for Management Systems in the Office of the Assistant Secretary of the Air Force for Financial Management. It claimed that this action was part of a broad effort to cut back staff for reasons of economy and was "absolutely not" related to what it referred to as Fitzgerald's "previous notoriety in relation with congressional testimony." Secretary of the Air Force Robert C. Seamans said that the job abolished was one of some 850 reductions in the service. However, there can be no doubt that the Air Force action was a reprisal for the testimony that Fitzgerald had given to our Subcommittee. The second method suggested in the January memo to accomplish Fitzgerald's departure—a "reduction in force"—had been used.

The firing was a clear message from the Pentagon to its employees: Do not try to reduce costs; do not aim at efficiency; do not attempt to achieve economy in government. The Pentagon has decided to control its cost-conscious employees rather than the costs of its programs. Its lame justification for firing Fitzgerald as an economy move made a mockery of that term.

Fitzgerald told the press, "My boss said they were eliminating my job in order to save money. If they really wanted to save money, we could save it elsewhere, by the bushels."

Insult was then added to injury. The Air Force hired John

J. Dyment, a thirty-six-year-old consultant from Arthur Young and Company at $107.92 a day to carry out some of Fitzgerald's old duties. This company was the auditor for Lockheed Aircraft and a party to a stockholders' suit charging that the company had hidden from stockholders the facts about the C-5A overrun. Judy Schedler, the wife of the new Assistant Secretary of the Air Force for Financial Management, Spencer J. Schedler, who hired Dyment and Arthur Young Company, was an $11,000-a-year employee of the Washington, D.C., branch of Arthur Young and Company. The Air Force subsequently dropped Dyment, but not until after public and press criticism had made it necessary. Fitzgerald was not reinstated, however.

An employee as dedicated and as loyal to the true interests of this nation deserves better treatment than to be drummed out of the government. But like the story of patriot John McGee, the story of patriot Ernie Fitzgerald has an unhappy ending.

If the Pentagon meant business in properly serving the nation, these heroes of the cost battles would be promoted. Instead, the defense Establishment seems intent on destroying its credibility with the American public, and on rendering itself incapable of doing an efficient, honest job, by crushing its most courageous and constructive critics. It is too bad. There are not enough government servants who view their duty as cost-cutting, not empire-building. And the Pentagon, of all government agencies, can least afford to lose one good man.

III

Blank Check for the Military

THE UNITED STATES could increase its military might by reducing funds available for military weapons. We could be more secure by spending less.

These statements may be hard to believe. But our present extravagant way of procuring weapons systems actually invites excessive costs, late deliveries, and abandoned projects. The long list of military weapons proposed and abandoned, the extraordinary cost overruns, the routinely late delivery schedules, and the failure of planes, tanks, guns, ships, and, especially, their electronic systems, to measure up to contract specifications amply prove the point. The evidence of massive failures is overwhelming. One need only read the record, beginning with the C-5A.

The saga of the C-5A began in 1961, when the Kennedy Administration was probing for an alternative to all-out nu-

clear war. The giant airplane was supposed to help provide a flexible response to small-scale or brush-fire wars, giving the United States an option beyond the Hobson's choice of nuclear attack or nothing. With such a plane, it was claimed, masses of equipment could be flown thousands of miles at short notice more efficiently and less expensively than with a number of smaller cargo planes.

The proposed transport required no great breakthrough in design or construction. It was a "state-of-the art" plane. But it was gigantic. It was so gigantic, in fact, that instead of being named for only one star or planet in the firmament, it was called the Galaxy. The original specifications called for a plane as big as a football field, which could carry 14 jet fighters, 50 cars, or 130,000 live lobsters. (Given the proclivities of the military to promote logistic support over combat strength, it is not clear whether, in an emergency, jet fighters or lobsters were to be airlifted to the world's trouble spots.)

Because of past deficiencies in getting orders filled, a new method of negotiating big contracts, called "total package procurement," was to be used for the C-5A. This was to prevent the excesses of the past, to which even the Air Force later admitted. The official Air Force Guidebook for May, 1966, stated:

> . . . the history of defense procurement was replete with cost overruns, less than promised performance, which were at least in part the result of intentional buy-in bidding, and this has been the case even in the situation where there has been no substantial increase in the then state of the art.

According to the Air Force, the new total-package method of contracting was "designed to check the large cost increases of the past."

After the go-ahead on the C-5A had been announced, a competition to develop the new plane ensued, with Lock-

heed, Boeing, and Douglas Aircraft as the key contenders for the Air Force contract.

An Air Force selection board gave Boeing the nod as having the best aircraft. But when Lockheed's bid was $330 million less than Boeing's, the board was reversed by the top Air Force echelon, including the military Chief of Staff John McConnell and civilian Secretary Eugene Zuckert.

Former Assistant Secretary of the Air Force for Installations and Logistics Robert Charles, who had conceived the "total-package procurement," negotiated the contract. He called it the "toughest ever made."

But once the contract was let, prices began to skyrocket. Overhead costs at Lockheed soared. Change orders further boosted costs. Soon they were far above the original estimate. As late as September, 1968, the Air Force was still telling Congress that costs were in line with early estimates, despite the fact that, a year earlier, in 1967, the Comptroller of the Pentagon had written to Secretary McNamara that the Air Force figures on the plane were wildly misleading. Worse, the Air Force's own internal official cost figures at that very time were $2 billion above the comparable 1965 estimates. A. E. Fitzgerald's November, 1968, testimony before the Subcommittee on Economy in Government of the Joint Economic Committee finally revealed the true figures. The 120 Galaxy C-5 planes and the spare parts for them would cost $5.33 billion. This was almost precisely $2 billion more than the $3.37 billion estimated in 1965 for the same plane.

Other facts soon came out. The plane was being produced by Lockheed at Air Force Plant No. 6 in Marietta, Georgia. This government–owned plant had an original acquisition cost of $113.8 million, which included 730 acres of land at an original cost of less than $400 an acre (now worth much more), improvements worth $74 million, and machinery and equipment for which the government had paid $39.6 million. Furthermore, Lockheed had received Air Force "progress

payments" of up to 90 per cent of the money it spent on the contract. Thus, the U.S. Government was supplying not only the plant and machinery but most of the company's working capital.

But the really big gimmick was a "repricing formula" that would only go into effect if the government exercised its option to buy the planes in the *second* of two production runs. The effect of this formula was to allow Lockheed to recoup on the second run a very large portion of the extra costs, which they would otherwise have had to absorb themselves. The repricing formula, later dubbed the "golden hand-shake," requires careful explanation. It is complicated, but an understanding of it is necessary in order to comprehend what was involved for the American taxpayer.

The Lockheed contract called for two production runs. In Run A, fifty-eight of the total of 120 planes were to be produced. The rest were reserved for Run B. Lockheed was responsible for, but was not actually producing, the engines; they were built elsewhere. The "target cost" for the fifty-eight airframes the company itself was building in Run A had been set at $800 million. These costs rose by $500 million to $1.3 billion—62.5 per cent more than originally targeted.

When Secretary Charles bragged that the contract was the "toughest" ever made by the Air Force, he was referring to the provision that Lockheed's profits would decrease as costs rose over the established "target cost" of $800 million. Moreover, if these costs went over a "target ceiling," Lockheed would lose money. This, Congress and the public were led to believe, would happen because of the $500 million cost overrun on the first batch of fifty-eight planes. But the situation was utterly different. What no one understood, except a few insiders, was that the repricing formula would bail out Lockheed if the second batch of planes, or Run B, was ordered by the Air Force.

The golden handshake provided a surefire means for Lock-

heed to recoup its losses. Under the contract's complicated
provisions, 30 points could be subtracted from the percentage
by which the actual costs exceeded the target costs; that
amount was to be multiplied by 2 to get the percentage by
which the target price on Run B would be raised. In this
case, $1.3 billion was 62.5 per cent more than the original
estimate of $800 million. Deduct the 30 points. Multiply this
figure of 32.5 by 2. The result is a new figure of 65 per cent.
This was the amount by which the costs on Run B could
legally be raised if the costs of Run A were excessive. In short,
the way it worked out, the higher the costs in Run A, the
more, by a multiplier of 2, the government was required to
pay for Run B!

The airframes for Run B had originally been estimated at
$490 million. By adding 65 per cent, the figure became $810
million or $320 more than the original estimate. This in-
crease under the repricing formula meant that, instead of
absorbing the losses on the first fifty-eight planes, Lockheed
would almost break even if Run B were authorized.

Thus, the go-ahead on Run B became a crucial decision.

Fitzgerald's testimony in November, 1968, had first brought
the C-5A overruns to public attention. His further testimony
on January 15, 1969, brought the whole story into sharper
focus. The losses on Run A were known. Even the first
five experimental planes had not then been produced. Delivery on the first production plane for the Air Force had
been postponed from July to December, 1969. With a $2 bil-
lion overrun, the original rationale—that it was cheaper to
buy one giant plane than several smaller planes—had dis-
appeared. There was every reason to postpone a decision on
Run B. For the first time, enormous cost overruns had been
spotted before a defense contract was finished and while
something might still be done about it.

Furthermore, as a report later issued by Charles's successor,
Assistant Secretary Philip N. Whittaker, brought out, the Air

Force needed to buy only forty C-5A planes to meet its special military requirements. The other eighty of the contracted-for total were to be used for all types of cargo requirements. At the new price, these nonessential planes were no bargain.

All told, there was no economic or military reason to proceed with Run B of the Lockheed contract. By canceling it altogether or by using it as a lever in negotiations to force Lockheed to reduce the excessive price on the planes in the second run, very important amounts could be saved for the taxpayers. Yet, instead of stopping with the first run, Assistant Secretary Charles and the Air Force gave Lockheed the go-ahead on Run B, two days before the Johnson Administration left office.

This bail-out led key members of Congress to dub the original Air Force agreement with Lockheed a "sweetheart contract." Some on the Senate Armed Services Committee voiced their suspicion that Lockheed had been guilty of "buying-in," or bidding low deliberately in order to get the contract. This wasteful procurement practice has always been one of the worst abuses under negotiated methods of military contracting. Change orders, revised specifications, and the cost-plus nature of contracts have always allowed the big companies to recapture their costs once a project was under way.

In addition, the C-5A was built in a government plant, where the company's investment was marginal. Costs rose. Delivery was delayed. Progress payments continued. Worst of all, the repricing formula wrote in an incentive to overcharge, since the greater the overrun on Run A, the more Lockheed benefited from the go-ahead on Run B. Critics also suspected that company officials originally hoped that the overrun on Run A would pay much of the cost for Lockheed to build a commercial version of the cargo plane. With only a small penalty against profits for the excessive costs on Run A, it could prove cheaper for Lockheed to milk the contract and sustain an overrun than to invest its own money for a nonmilitary C-5A. All the built-in incentives were on the side of overcharging the U.S. Government.

Under public criticism, Assistant Secretary Charles and the Air Force soon devised their excuses for the outlandish terms of the contract, for the extraordinary increase in costs, and for the unbelieveable decision—in light of the public disclosures—to proceed with Run B.

Excuse number one: The increase in price was only $1.2 billion, not almost $2 billion.

Excuse number two: Two different planes were being compared. The existing C-5A was a bigger plane than the original C-5A, it was alleged, and most of the cost was due to that fact.

Excuse number three: Inflation was the cause of $500 million of the total.

An interesting euphemism appeared among the Air Force excuses. The term "cost overrun" became "cost growth."

But Assistant Secretary Charles was off base with all of his excuses. First of all, he used the original 1964 Air Force estimates in his figuring. These estimates were for a plane that was never produced. Then he failed to include the spare parts estimate, although it was given in the original figures. By starting from the wrong base and omitting the spare parts replacement figure, which itself jumped from $307 million to $855 million, he concluded that the total increase had been from $3.1 billion to $4.3 billion, or $1.2 billion.

The only proper method of judging the cost overrun (and it is based on exactly the same C-5A plane, not two different planes as Charles alleged in his second excuse) is to compare the 1965 Air Force estimate for the plane sought at the time the contract was let with the official Air Force figures for October, 1968. This comparison shows an increase in costs, including the $500 million jump in replenishment of spare parts, from an original April, 1965, estimate of $3.371 billion to $5.330 billion—a jump of $1.959 billion.* That is as close to an overrun of $2 billion as I care to get.

A fundamental question remains. Do we need more than forty of these planes at this cost? Stopping Run B would at least have cut the losses. A major aerospace company, for the first time, would have had to bear the burden of its inefficiency. Forcing a contractor to absorb his own losses would help bring efficiency to Pentagon procurement.

Overruns and other abuses are not limited to Air Force projects alone. Excesses on the C-5A contract are matched by the Army in the procurement of new tanks.

The Army's Sheridan tank is a small 16-ton assault vehicle with light aluminum armor. The Army was so anxious to get this tank into action that it sent sixty of them to Vietnam and manufactured and stored hundreds more before the tank itself or the 152mm. gun it carried was perfected.

The first big problem was with the guns. When conventional weapons are fired, gunners must remove the brass shell casing after each round. The proposed 152mm. gun for the Sheridan tank fired an advanced type of ammunition with a cartridge or casing that is supposed to burn up in the gun breech. But the combustible shell did not burn up completely. The remaining residue ignited and detonated the shell loaded next, causing serious problems for the men firing the weapons.

The Army rushed into mass production long before the ammunition-system problem was solved, arguing that it was necessary to push production of the tank itself because of the long lead-time involved. When asked by Congressman Sam-

* Tables prepared by my staff and printed in the *Congressional Record* for September 4, 1969, are reproduced at the back of this book. They show the actual breakdown in millions of dollars for the full C-5A program growth, the unit costs derived from the program estimates, and the unit costs (excluding spare parts) for Lockheed only.

uel S. Stratton, of New York, why it moved ahead this way, the Army replied, "We would have had ammunition running out our ears."

"Instead," Congressman Stratton shot back, "you have tanks running out your ears."

Congressman Stratton thought there was another reason why the Army pushed ahead after spending $1.5 billion on the tank's new weapons system without effective results: to prevent higher-ups in the Department of Defense from cutting off funds for the tank. He produced an Army document saying that the action was ordered so that attention would not be focused "unnecessarily" on the tank program, which, it was said, would place it "in jeopardy of cancellation." Stratton was backed up by a confidential General Accounting Office report that accused the Army of rushing the program to avoid "adverse political and budgetary impacts."

As a result of the Army's haste, neither the weapons nor the tank worked properly. Deployed in Vietnam before final field tests were held, the Sheridan tanks were beset with problems. They made so much noise that they could be heard three miles away—obviously, an unsatisfactory feature for combat troops, whose lives depend on surprise. The engines overheated, because heavy vegetation clogged the air intake tubes and the small radiators. To function, these needed periodic cleaning. But troops in combat were reluctant to climb out of the vehicle and clean them every hour on the hour. Army Lieutenant General Austin Betts, the chief of Army Research and Development, told a House committee that in combat the troops "would get impatient about cleaning the filters and bang them on things to shake the dust out of them."

The difficulties, the General said, "were mostly related to the fact that in combat crews are not as careful with their equipment as they are in a peacetime testing environment."

Failure to field test the tank under simulated combat conditions before deployment in Vietnam contributed to other problems, which did not result from careless handling by harassed soldiers. The fuel tanks leaked. They did not merely spill fuel on the ground, but the fuel leaked inside the tank, where it could cause burning infernos. Understated new instructions were issued advising the crews to check for spilled fuel to prevent fires. The tank had no range finder for its weapons. Its night-vision periscope often failed. Above speeds of fifteen miles per hour, the tank shook so hard that its functioning was affected even on hard-surfaced roads. During combat, troops also used it as a battering ram, although its sixteen tons were too light to perform that function successfully. All in all, some twenty-five pages of restrictions on its use were written.

Congressman Stratton had considerable justification when he called the Sheridan a "billion-dollar boo-boo."

But the problems of the light sixteen-ton Sheridan tank were only a curtain raiser to the troubles that beset the huge main battle tank, called the MBT-70, which weighs three to four times as much as the Sheridan.

The MBT was originally conceived in 1963 as a joint project with West Germany. The two nations agreed to split the $86 million development cost. It was scheduled to roll off the production lines in 1969 and was to be a more maneuverable, less vulnerable tank with more firepower—including both 152mm. cartridges and the Shillelagh missile through a single tube mounted on the tank—than its predecessors. It was designed to fight in a nuclear or biologically contaminated area.

But costs on the MBT skyrocketed while delays in production increased. By 1965, the research and development costs had grown to $138 million. West Germany limited its share to only half of that amount. Above $138 million, each country would contribute according to the number of tanks it bought. In July, 1968, the cost had risen to $303 million. Soon, the U.S. research and development cost alone ran to

$277 million. The West Germans called a halt, saying that they had had enough. Meantime, the delivery date was delayed to 1974. The cost per unit grew to $600,000 to $750,000 each, compared with a unit cost of $250,000 for the M-60 tank, the MBT's predecessor.

But costs and delays are only part of the problem. The main question with the MBT-70 is, "Do we need the tank at all?"

The strategic projections for the MBT made in 1963 and covering a period through 1969 were based on the assumption that we must be prepared to fight a tactical nuclear war on the continent of Europe. Even in 1963 that was a doubtful assumption. Was there then or is there now really any possibility that tactical nuclear weapons could be fired at invading forces in the center of Europe without escalating the conflict into a nuclear holocaust? To assume otherwise appears ridiculous. This tank has suffered long production delays, encountered numerous technical difficulties, and costs too much. Its Shillelagh weapon system does not work. Its protection against nuclear fallout is no greater than that of the M-60. Worse, it is highly vulnerable to new anti-tank weapons (infantrymen can now knock out a tank with a guided missile fired from a bazooka-like weapon). Yet, this tank was justified originally on strategically impossible grounds. Could it really be used to lob small atomic weapons across the Rhine? Could it be used to defend Berlin against an East German siege? In what way would it deter a Russian invasion of the West if our Poseidon and Minuteman missiles had not already deterred them?

The truth is that unless there is an all-out nuclear war, this tank would never fire or resist tactical nuclear weapons in the center of Europe. And if an all-out war occurred, the tank would be useless in any case. The MBT is not only a technical failure. It is a strategic stupidity.

There are many other examples of such indefensible procurement. The list of cost overruns, unneeded or abandoned projects, and malfunctioning weapons is almost endless. To describe a few:

—The Air Force's MOL program, the acronym for Manned Orbiting Laboratory, was scrubbed on June 10, 1969, after expenditures of $1.3 billion and estimated costs had risen from $2 to $3 billion. At the time it was ended, technical delays had postponed the first manned flight from December 1969 to mid-1972 or nine years after its conception and seven years after the program began. Moreover, it duplicated a project of the National Aeronautics and Space Administration (NASA).

—The cost of the Navy's deep sea submarine rescue vessel increased from $3 million to over $77 million a unit or by more than 25 times. But its fundamental need is questioned. In all the submarine accidents since the 1920's, it could have made a difference only twice.

—Testimony before the Joint Economic Committee's Subcommittee on Economy in Government indicated that the cost of the Minuteman II missile increased from $3 to $7 billion. In one year, the costs of the SRAM, the short-range air-launched missile to be carried by the B-52 bomber and the FB-111 fighter bomber, rose from $300 to $600 million. In addition, the estimated costs for 800 of the Mark II electronic brains for the F-111 fighter plane soared from $600 million to $2.5 billion—an increase of $1.9 billion or 300 per cent—and the performance standards for the "black boxes" were greatly reduced and the contract ceiling costs greatly increased after the Autonetics Division of North American Aviation admitted that there were more than 600 defects in the original F-111 brain it bid to produce.

—The Air Force, the Atomic Energy Commission, and the Navy spent over $1 billion in a futile attempt to build an airplane powered by atomic energy. The project was abandoned.

—The Army wasted $60 million on 60 atomic cannons. Only three are still extant. The other 57 were sold for junk.

—When two prototypes of the Navy's Seamaster jet-propelled flying boat crashed, the Navy abandoned this project to build a mine-laying plane. The cost was $361 million.

—When costs for the Army's Cheyenne helicopter almost doubled from $1.5 million to just under $3 million each, while the technical troubles with its rigid-rotor technology remained unsolved, the contract with Lockheed was halted. One of the ten prototypes crashed, and, according to a military trade journal, the test flight was made, "despite a specific warning given to Lockheed days before the accident that the proposed flights could be catastrophic." Cited specifically in the Army's "cure notice" to Lockheed Aircraft were the "critical unstable rotor oscillations" of the rigid rotor system, as well as "rotor instabilities," "inadequate directional control," "excessive lift-roll and pitch-roll coupling during maneuvering" and too much weight which the Army's notice said could endanger the craft's "performance, maneuver capability and structural integrity." The total cost of the program, including research and development, was $1.06 billion. (Like the C-5A contract, the contract for the Cheyenne helicopter was let under the "total package procurement" method of negotiation.)

There are other failures—even more expensive and dangerous than any we have listed.

In the past, planes, tanks, and guns were the key to defense. In the new era, it is the computers, the radars, and the gyroscopes that are the crucial components of our defense and weapons systems. In the new weapons, the "avionics" systems —the term for the computers, radars, and gyroscopes—are the key to performance. The failure of these electronic brains to function are among the most shocking revelations made public in recent years.

Richard A. Stubbing is a 39-year-old, high-level (Grade

14) civil servant at the Budget Bureau. His job has been to examine the Pentagon's requests for funds. In 1966, he received the Budget Bureau Director's Professional Award for "outstanding achievement as an examiner in the military division and for unusual capacity in analysis of broad ranging programs and management problems." The next year, he was selected to attend the Woodrow Wilson School at Princeton as one of the government's outstanding career civil servants. While there, he wrote a lengthy paper entitled "Improving the Acquisition Process for High Risk Military Electronics Systems," which revealed a scandalous situation. The electronic systems on many major weapons did not work. Among the key findings in his paper were the following:

Of thirteen major aircraft and missile programs with sophisticated electronic systems built for the Air Force and the Navy since 1955, only four, costing $5 billion, could be relied upon to reach a performance level of 75 per cent or above of their required specifications.

Five more were poor performers and broke down at a performance level which was 75 per cent or less than their required specifications. These systems cost $13 billion.

Two more, costing $10 billion, were dropped within three years because of "low reliability."

Two more, costing $2 billion, were canceled.

The performance levels were based on the requirements of the contracts themselves. If, for example, the specifications called for the electronic brain in the Minuteman missile to function for 100 hours without a breakdown, it got a rating of 100 per cent if it met that requirement. It it ran only fifty hours before a breakdown occurred, its performance rating was 50 per cent. Reliable performance of the avionics for the new sophisticated missiles and planes are the key to their vital functioning. If they fail, the whole system fails.

Stubbing then examined a dozen programs started in the 1950's. They included such well-known airborne weapons systems as the F-4 fighter plane, the B-52 bomber, and the B-47, the F-102, F-100, and the F-104.

The performance record of the electronic systems in the twelve programs that were begun during that decade show that only five performed up to specifications or better. One more performed at the 75 per cent level. Four were at 50 per cent. Two more met only 25 per cent of the performance level called for in their original specifications.

If the programs begun in the 1950's were bad, those started in the decade of the 1960's were worse. The performance record of eleven major systems started in the 1960's show only two that performed up to standard. One more met a 75 per cent performance level. Two met a 50 per cent rate. But six, or over half of them, performed at only 25 per cent of the standards specified in the contract. In other words, if these six were supposed to function for 100 hours without failure, they broke down in 25 hours or less.

These shocking revelations about electronic airplane and missile systems that do not perform one-quarter or one-half or three-quarters of the time were first brought to public attention by Bernard Nossiter, whose reporting of military procurement in the *Washington Post* is unsurpassed by that of any newspaperman in the country. They raise new questions about the basic reliability of our weapons. In the past, military experts and systems managers have bragged about "more bang for a buck." Are we approaching the time when we will get no bang for a buck?

Nossiter's article on Stubbing revealed additional shocking facts about weapons-systems and avionics procurement. Among them are that the ten highest profits go to what appear to be the most inefficient firms.

In the period 1957–66, North American Aviation did 98 per cent of its business with the government. In those years, it produced seven major weapons. One plane built in the mid-1950's was highly successful. Another met its performance standards. A third system was canceled. The remaining four systems broke down four times as often as their specifications called for. Yet, according to the Stubbing study, North American's after-tax profits based on its investment were 40 per cent above those of the aerospace industry and 50 per cent above those for industry as a whole.

General Dynamics, which had seven dubious results out of seven starts, including the ill-fated TFX, had an uneven profit record for the decade. But its poor years were those when it engaged in building a commercial plane. When it was working for the Pentagon, the company fared well despite its shut-out record.

The aerospace industry as a whole, measured by its performance on electronic weapons systems, was among the most inefficient in the country. Yet, during the decade from 1957 to 1966 it had after-tax earnings on investment that were 12.5 per cent or one-eighth higher than American industry as a whole.

In addition to the low level of performance and the high level of profits, complex electronic systems typically cost 200 to 300 per cent more than the Pentagon estimates. On the average, they are delivered two years late.

The world of the military-industrial complex is an upside-down, Alice-in-Wonderland world.

In a competitive industrial society, one would expect that high profits would go to those companies whose performance exceeded expectations, whose costs were under those anticipated, and whose delivery schedules were met or beaten. Not so in the case of weapons-systems contractors. Here we have high profits without performance. Rewards are in reverse relationship to the time taken and the funds spent. Failures are rewarded and minimum standards are seldom met. Prices soar, profits rise, but contracts continue. And the taxpayer holds the bag.

But excessive costs are not the only concern. This matter

must also be examined from the viewpoint of the security of our country. Criticism of financial excesses and fumbling performances is sometimes equated, unpardonably, with a new isolationism or a lack of confidence in the country. The opposite is true. Waste weakens us. The country and its military defense are far better served by close scrutiny, public criticism, and some canceled contracts.

However, to keep a close check on military expenditures in the United States today is not easy. The fate of the Stubbing study shows why. Since its publication, Stubbing has generally been unavailable for comment. He has become one of the most anonymous men in Washington.

At a Defense Department news conference, Secretary of Defense Melvin R. Laird dismissed Stubbing's findings and his work as a "graduate study—graduate thesis." He criticized the measurement of reliability that Stubbing used to judge performance and claimed that the important matter was whether a new weapon outperformed its predecessor (apparently, regardless of the additional cost) or met its specifications. He declined to talk about the central fact that fourteen of twenty-three major weapons systems operate at only half their contract performance-requirements or, put the other way around, break down twice as fast as their specifications require. He also dismissed the study on the grounds that, because it has not been classified, it is unimportant.

According to published reports, Secretary Laird also suggested that public discussion of the breakdown of our weapons system might shake the faith of our potential enemies in the reliability of our weapons systems. This lack of credibility might then fail to deter the enemy to the degree the system was designed to do. He also said that the effect of public discussion might weaken the position of our negotiators in any arms-limitations talks.

Time and again in the debate over the ABM, arguments

like these were heard. The overwhelming scientific evidence that the radar, computer, and communications systems, of the ABM would not work under attack because they could not be "hardened" and, hence, were highly vulnerable to attack was dismissed. We were told that the important matter was not whether the systems worked but whether a potential enemy thought they worked. Time and again we were told that the enemy has to assume that the systems will function, whether they actually function or not. To point out their failures, however undeniable, was to weaken our defense and to destroy the credibility of our deterrence. In this kind of ridiculous upside-down world, it doesn't matter whether the weapons work or not. What is important is to make an enemy think they work.

Time and time again we have been told that we must buy some billion-dollar gadget, not because the Soviet Union has one, or even that it is beginning production on one, but merely because the Russians have the "capability" to build one.

The failures of the electronic and avionic systems in the major weapons we have developed are outweighed by the billions of dollars spent for intercontinental and submarine-launched ballistic missiles (ICBM's and SLBM's) abandoned in the research and development stage or before they were ever finished. It is a fantastic list of missiles named for Greek Gods, celestial bodies, Indian tribes, ancient weapons, birds, and animals. (Occasionally, a public relations man comes up with a brainstorm and an acronym like GAM is added to the list.) Many, many billions more have been lost on missile systems that were planned, produced, deployed, and then abandoned.

The Army spent $399 million on the Hermes, Dart, Loki, and the land-based Terrier, Plato, and Mauler. It abandoned them all before deployment.

The Navy spent two and one half times the money on

twice as many weapons before they abandoned a dozen of
them costing $993 million. Included were Sparrows I and II,
Regulus II, Petrel, Corvus, Eagle, Meteor, Rigel, Dove, Tri-
ton, Oriole, and Typhon.

The Air Force abandoned at least ten missiles before they
were deployed. True to form, they spent three times as much
on two fewer missiles as did the Navy. The Navaho and
Snark were abandoned after expenditures of $1.35 billion.
Their problem was that they were "air-breathing" intercontinental missiles. They could fly at the speed of sound and
reach Europe from the northern bases in the United States,
but they were incapable of leaving the earth's atmosphere
because their jets could not function without air. Rascal and
Skybolt were canceled after costs of $888 million. Others
abandoned after smaller losses included the Drone, Goose,
Crossbow and Talos. The Air Force's expenditures on missiles abandoned before they were ever deployed totaled
about $2.8 billion.

The billions spent on missiles actually produced and deployed before they were scrapped include a total of $4.1 bil-
lion the Army spent—more than half of it, or $2.26 billion,
on the Nike-Ajax missiles and sites. The Navy, less extravagant than her sister services, abandoned only the Polaris I,
after expenditures of $1.13 billion, and the Regulus, at the
modest price of $413 million, for a total cost of $1.54 billion The Air Force won all the blue ribbons for high costs
and low efficiency. Various versions of the Atlas and Titan
cost the country $8.6 of the $13.2 billion the Air Force spent
on deployed and then abandoned missiles. Others included
Thor, at $1.4 billion, Bomarc, at $1.4 billion, and Jupiter,
Hound Dog A, and Mace A, for the remaining $1.08 billion.

Altogether, the services spent a grand total of $4.1 billion
on twenty-eight systems abandoned before deployment and
$18.9 billion on fifteen more abandoned after deployment.

We have reviewed the C-5A, the Sheridan tank, and the MBT-70, the missile failures, and other costly, unsuccessful programs in our recital of the excesses on which the military has spent the blank check handed it by Congress and the American people. There is still another story of foolish extravagance to be told.

The Pentagon has a penchant for naming its weapons for Greek or Norse Gods or for characters from Wagnerian operas. The ill-fated Valkyrie experimental bomber (XB-70) is merely one in a long list of weapons so named. But the Air Force version of the Valkyrie, instead of roaming the heavens determining the outcome of battles, as did the mythological Norse maiden, now rests, forever grounded, at the Air Force Museum in Dayton, Ohio—far away from Norwegian fiords or Rhine River rapids.

Started in 1954, with a small $500,000 appropriation, the Valkyrie ended fifteen years later, after expenditures of almost $2 billion. Instead of the 200 V-shaped, swept-winged bombers, which look like a child's paper airplane, only two XB-70's were ever built. The sister version of the plane now at Dayton crashed, ironically, on a flight undertaken for public relations purposes, when air currents swept a trailing fighter plane into its tail stabilizers and caused it to nosedive into the earth.

From the beginning, the big plane was plagued with cost and technical problems. In 1964, ten years and $1.5 billion after it began, the first plane had not been assembled. Designed to fly at 70,000 feet and at 2,000 miles per hour, it had not yet left the ground. While the Air Force pressed for its deployment against the opposition of Secretary Mc-Namara, Congress consistently authorized more funds than the President or the Secretary were willing to spend. When the program was cut from three planes to two in 1964, Secretary McNamara and almost everyone but the Air Force and their congressional supporters argued that a new manned bomber in an age of sophisticated missiles was a technical, tactical, and strategic anomaly.

Yet today, while one XB-70 forlornly rests at the Dayton museum, the Air Force and the industrial-propaganda combine, dependent on its handouts of tax dollars, are attempting to resurrect a new and equally costly version of the XB-70 from the ashes of the other Valkyrie that plunged into the California desert.

Unwilling to give up, the Air Force has routinely pressed for a new manned bomber. Just as routinely, the Kennedy and Johnson administrations limited expenditures to the research and development phase of the proposed new weapon system. But, on the grounds that we need a "strategic mix" to supplement our land-based and submarine missile force, Secretary Laird in March, 1969, asked for an additional $23 million to move a new advanced manned strategic aircraft (AMSA) from the research to the design and prototype production stage.

Just before he left office, in January, 1969, former Secretary of Defense Clark Clifford outlined the strategic situation in the annual posture statement presented to the Senate Armed Services Committee. In his statement on the proposed 1970 defense budget, Secretary Clifford said the United States had 646 intercontinental bombers compared to only 150 for the Russians. These are the heavy bombers that can fly two-way intercontinental missions. The Secretary pointed out in a footnote that the Russians also have a force of medium bombers and tankers capable of striking European and Asian targets.

But, Secretary Clifford said, "The estimate of the Soviet manned bomber force is essentially the same as presented last year. There is still no evidence that the Soviets intend to deploy a new heavy bomber in the early 1970's." And he added: "Their Bison and Bear long-range bombers are distinctly inferior to our B-52's and we have long since eliminated from our forces the B-47's which were clearly superior to their Badger medium bombers."

At that time, there was absolutely no evidence that the Russians either had or were planning to build new strategic bombers that either could rival or surpass our existing force. If anything, the raw numbers exaggerated the strength of the Russians, considering the relative inferiority of their force. The United States has an overwhelming superiority both in quantity and quality of manned bombers.

But when Secretary Laird came before the Senate Armed Services Committee on March 19, 1969, he said in his "new" posture statement that the Pentagon had decided to cut off the FB-111 program at four squadrons and concentrate its efforts on the development of the new AMSA. Laird further testified that the fiscal 1970 budget of the outgoing administration provided $77.2 million to continue the AMSA's competitive design phase—engineering drawings, wind-tunnel testing, and mockups—and to advance the development of the long-lead–time avionics and propulsion system.

Then, in what was a highly significant and, at that time, little noticed—sentence, Secretary Laird stated: "We now propose to increase that amount by $23 million to shorten the competitive design phase and permit the start of a full scale engineering development in fiscal year 1970."

This seemed to mean that the Air Force was now definitely going ahead with the AMSA. It appeared that by adding $23 million, they were on their way. If they reached the so-called contract definition stage with the added $23 million, they would then build at least one prototype at a cost certainly in the neighborhood of $1.5 to $2 billion. We were told that the Air Force planned to build 240 planes. It was said the estimated cost was $50 million per plane.

Considering that the C-5A cargo plane will cost at least $40 million a plane and that the original estimates for the supersonic transport were from $30 to $40 million a plane, the AMSA seems to be on the low side. After all, a supersonic, high- and low-level bomber not only must carry the same sophisticated instrumentation as a supersonic civilian plane but also must carry the highly complex weapon system instrumentation as well. Estimates from other than official Air Force sources are, therefore, as high as $80 million per plane.

These higher, and probably far more accurate, estimates mean that by the addition of a small amount—$23 million— this year, we are essentially committed to at least a $12 billion program.

This is almost double the original estimate of the cost of the ABM program, about which there has been such controversy. And the final total could go much higher.

The added $23 million, according to the Secretary, "could advance the initial operation capability of this aircraft by one year from 1978 to 1977." In other words, $23 million now would mean delivery of the fleet in 1977. But the history of both costs and delivery dates for major weapons systems is such that they routinely are delivered two to three years late and at costs greatly exceeding estimates. We are probably talking about a fleet of 240 planes that will be delivered a decade from now at a cost of at least $20 billion —and may be obsolete before they fly.

The fundamental question is whether we should build a manned bomber in an age of sophisticated missile systems. In 1962, the President and the then Secretary of Defense resisted an expensive addition of manned bombers. Secretary Laird has said that the AMSA would be operational in 1977, or fifteen years after the highest officials of our government challenged the need for an additional generation of manned bombers.

But this action on the AMSA raised other important questions.

What effect will the decision to go ahead have on the arms race?

Will not the Russians feel compelled to increase the number of their bombers, or to build up the defensive system needed to cope with our new bomber, or to improve their offensive weapons, or all three? In turn, will not the Military Establishment in this country argue that, because the Russians have increased their proportionate effort, we must also increase the expenditures of our resources for additional weapons to meet their new threat?

Unless new overwhelming evidence is produced, the development of the AMSA should be stopped. This request is an example of the operation of the military-industrial complex at its worst.

Even the late 1969 leaks from the Air Force that the Russians are testing a new F-111-like, swing-wing bomber should not stampede us into headlong production of a new supersonic intercontinental bomber. The Russian plane is a medium bomber with a limited 2,500-mile range. It raises more questions about the efficiency of our intelligence than it threatens the security of the United States. Even if it is built, the United States would still be far ahead.

For us to build an expensive new manned bomber is a waste of our resources, an example of misplaced priorities, and a threat to our own safety and security. Not only will its cost be immense but, by so devoting funds to obsolete weapons, we enfeeble our military strength and make the nation less, rather than more, secure.

Shortly after Secretary Laird had announced that the Air Force was planning "full-scale engineering development" on the AMSA, alarmed by the implications of his announcement, I wrote to him asking a series of questions on this subject. Six weeks passed by. Late one afternoon, the Pentagon delivered to my office an envelope marked "Secret." When I inquired as to its contents, I was told that it was a reply to my

letter on the AMSA. Within minutes, I called the Defense
Department, insisted that a messenger be sent to my office,
and returned the envelope unopened.

I had intended to take the AMSA issue to the Senate floor.
By classifying "secret" the answers to my questions, the Pentagon could have made it impossible for me to speak freely. It
is one of the means the military planners regularly use to
deter criticism of their programs. I refused to fall into their
trap and demanded instead an unclassified reply to my
question.

Soon I received such a letter. To my mind, it answered my
original questions fully. Very few classified items are really
essential knowledge in making fundamental judgments
about military weapons. Much of what is kept secret are the
mistakes of the Pentagon, such as its reluctance to admit the
huge cost overruns on the C-5A airplane.

The stamp marked "secret" is one of three readily identi-
fiable psychological weapons that the military develops to
gain the upper hand in strategic argument. It is one of the
great Pentagon rationalizations brought out of reserve whenever military judgment is challenged. I call it the "if-you-
only-knew-what-I-know" ploy.

Another favorite is the "scare-hell-out-of-'em" syndrome.
Whenever the military hegemony is threatened, this argument is brought forward as the Army might order its mobile
reserves to the front at the critical moment of battle. It is the
argument that produced a missile gap where none existed. It
created a Russian long-range-supersonic-bomber threat where
none existed. It inspired the March 21, 1969, statement of
Defense Secretary Laird that "the Soviets are going for a first
strike capability, and no doubt about it," which he used as a
key argument in the battle over deployment of the ABM.
(Later, pressed to prove that the Russians either now or in
the foreseeable future would have the weapons to destroy our
ICBM's, our attack submarines and SLBM's, and our fleet of

long-range bombers, Laird demurred. A Russian first-strike capability meant only the potential to destroy our land-based ICBM's, he said. But, by definition, that is no first strike at all. Our 41 attack submarines with their 16 Polaris and Poseidon missiles, the latter to carry 10 weapons, could shower 4,000 to 5,000 nuclear warheads on any nation so rash as to order a strike at our ICBM's.)

Throughout the 1969 ABM debate, there were almost daily warnings from the Pentagon of the scare-hell-out-of-'em type, subclassification "the-Russians-will-get-you-if-you-don't-watch-out." If we had scuttled the fleet, blown up our planes and bombs, demobilized the Army, and destroyed our missiles, such dire warnings might have had the Muse of History at their side. But with our in-place strategic retaliatory power, they were plainly only the usual Pentagon rationalization of military plans.

Still another ploy regularly used by the Pentagon is the "foot-in-the-door" technique. As we have seen, the military services routinely open the way to huge expenditures by adding small sums to the research and development money for "contract definition," or prototypes, thereby ensuring a commitment for the eventual outlay of much, much larger funds. When objections to the larger amounts are raised at a later date, DOD spokesmen piously point to the seed sums as evidence that Congress authorized the effort.

The unclassified reply to my inquiries about the AMSA, signed by Dr. John S. Foster, Director of Research and Engineering for the Department of Defense, admitted as much. Dr. Foster said that the original $23 million involved in this project would trigger an expenditure of at least $1.8 billion for the production of prototypes, or test models.

He also said that if the planes went into production, they would cost about $25 to $30 million each in quantities of 200 or more. The total cost would be about $8 billion for both the prototypes and the production of 200 planes. Greater emphasis on research and engineering and the production of prototypes of most weapon systems could save billions of dollars, but this estimate of $1.8 billion, or 20 per cent of the total cost of 200 planes, for the prototypes seemed exceptionally high. Surely, this part of the job should be done for less money and more efficiently. But the estimate of only $25–$30 million each for the final plane is impossible to believe.

Once again, the Pentagon appears to be grossly underestimating the ultimate costs of a weapon system. It looks like the biggest yet in a long list of underestimated costs on a major weapons system. In my opinion, it is unrealistic, unreliable, and unattainable.

Is the Pentagon once again misleading the public and Congress about ultimate costs in order to get a new weapons system under way? The pressure for production of the AMSA rising out of the ashes of the Valkyrie is an example of how powerful the military-industrial complex is. Weapon systems once started seem to be like the Latin word *ait*—present, imperfect, impossible to decline, and having no future.

If these planes are to be used for conventional warfare, what can they do that a B-52 cannot do that justifies $1.8 billion for development and $10 to $20 billion as a minimum for production?

And, to ask the basic question once again, why do we need a new manned bomber in the missile age? If its strategic function is given as the reason for its production, what can a bomber possibly do that a missile cannot do better and cheaper?

The defenders of the military-industrial complex argue that we must not criticize our weapons systems, the decisions of the Pentagon, or the performance of contractors even when that criticism is true. If we do, they say, we will shake the faith of our enemies in the reliability of our weapons. It is on such grounds of "national security," as determined by the Pentagon, that information that should be made public is stamped "secret." It is on these grounds that the patriotism of those who criticize it is sometimes called into question.

This attack made by DOD and other officials on the patriotism of critics of the military-industrial complex and all its works is the most underhanded of all the psychological weapons in the Pentagon arsenal.

The United States is better served by the truth than by sweeping unhappy facts under the rug. It may sound absurd to say such a thing, but surely we are stronger if our weapons work than if they do not work. We are more secure facing facts and subjecting Pentagon actions to criticism than covering up the problems—and there are many more of them than the horrible examples described in this chapter.

The frightening truth about our weapons procurement system is that one can search in vain for a weapon that was produced on time, worked according to its specifications, and did not exceed the estimated cost.

Even when they work, which is rare indeed, weapons systems cost far too much and are delivered many years late.

Why this happens and what can be done about it are matters that need detailed examination and urgent action.

IV

Budget Review:
Ask Not the Reason Why

WEST OF THE WHITE HOUSE, on Pennsylvania Avenue, stands an enormous gray building in the ornate style of the French Renaissance and erected nearly a hundred years ago. Once it was known as the State, War, and Navy Building. Now it goes by the title of Executive Office Building. The State Department has new quarters in Foggy Bottom. The unified military services are quartered across the Potomac in the Pentagon. But what happens, or doesn't happen, in that old State, War, and Navy Building still directly affects American defense and foreign policies.

The building now houses top officials of the agency that is the right arm of the President and the U.S. Government's only "nay"-sayer, the Bureau of the Budget. Its functions determine the over-all size of the defense budget, how efficiently the Pentagon operates, and the priorities between military and civilian demands, as well as those within both the military and civilian categories.

Over the last two decades, the Budget Bureau has treated the Pentagon with kid gloves. It has granted the military a privileged status in the government. Instead of facing up to Pentagon pressures and forcing its will on the military, the Bureau of the Budget has approached the Defense Department subserviently, hat in hand. Sitting in their high-ceilinged offices in that old State, War, and Navy Building, the otherwise diligent officials of the Budget Bureau have failed, as far as spending for national defense is concerned, to exercise their responsibilities.

In the first place, the Budget Bureau has failed to assign adequate personnel to examine the military budget. Whereas funds for foreign aid, the poverty program, education, or urban development are gone over with a fine-tooth comb, the military budget has escaped effective examination. As much as any single factor, this accounts for "the unwarranted influence of the military-industrial complex," the power of the Pentagon, and burgeoning military spending.

The discrepancy in treatment of civilian and military departments was admitted by former Budget Bureau officials who appeared before the Subcommittee on Economy in Government of the Joint Economic Committee early in 1969. When asked pointedly if, under his administration, the Defense Department's budget was scrutinized as carefully, dollar for dollar, as those of the departments of Health, Education, and Welfare, and Housing and Urban Development, former Budget Director Charles Zwick replied: "Defense is a big department. We obviously do not get into as great detail in that department as we do in some other departments."

Yet a dollar saved at the Pentagon is worth just as much as a dollar saved at HUD or from the poverty program or anywhere else.

Why the DOD budget is not looked at in the same detail as others was developed further when Robert P. Mayo, President Nixon's Budget Director, testified before our Subcommittee shortly after Zwick's appearance. I pointed out and Mayo agreed that, of the budget outlays of approximately $180 billion, huge amounts are relatively fixed. Unless fundamental legislative changes are made, these costs, called uncontrollable outlays, are automatically paid out. Among the most important are social security, Medicare, interest on the national debt, veterans' pensions and programs, Commodity Credit Corporation payments, and outlays under contracts and obligations wherein the full faith and credit of the United States have been pledged. These uncontrollable items add up to over $80 billion a year.

That leaves only $100 billion of "controllable" budget items—the amount that the President, the Budget Bureau, and Congress can affect. Almost $80 of the $100 billion of controllable items go for national defense. They include the defense budget and those parts of the space and atomic energy budgets that involve defense outlays.

The Budget Bureau employs about 500 professional people. According to Director Mayo's testimony, no more than 50 of the 500 have been assigned to examine the defense budget. On the face of it, this means that only 10 per cent of the key budget personnel have examined 80 per cent of the $100 billion in controllable budget items, while the other 90 per cent scrutinized only 20 per cent of the funds. However, because of the hundreds of minor-line items in the federal budget—which, as a published document, exceeds the Manhattan phone book in size and weight—the actual assignment of personnel was perhaps not as distorted in effect as these numbers might indicate. For example, it takes almost as much effort to examine the details of the Battle Monument Commission's tiny budget as it does to look at the Civil Division of the Justice Department, which may spend many times as much. A fairer estimate of the percentage of Budget Bureau employees engaged in reviewing military spending might raise the figure from 10 per cent to 15 or 20 per cent. (Deputy Budget Director Phillip S. Hughes's estimate before a House committee of 25 per cent seems a bit too generous.)

Even so, Zwick's concession that the Budget Bureau failed to "get into as great a detail in that department as we do in some other departments" is the understatement of the fiscal year. To paraphrase Gertrude Stein, a dollar is a dollar is a dollar.

Not only has the Budget Bureau failed to assign sufficient examiners to the Defense Department, but other of its past procedures also have differed fundamentally from those followed by the rest of the departments and agencies of government. As Congressman William Moorhead observed, "The Budget Bureau trembles before the Defense Department while all other agencies tremble before the Budget Bureau."

When civilian department budgets are reviewed, the Budget Bureau examiner sits as judge over the proceedings. The departments come to him. He does the reviewing on his own home grounds and then makes recommendations to the Director. Appeals against his decision are made by the departments to the Budget Bureau. Even in the most important matters, where the clash reaches the President, the Cabinet officer must appeal to the President to overturn the decision of the Budget Director.

Until very recently, this procedure was not followed by the Budget Bureau in dealing with the Pentagon. Hearing examiners marched out of the old State, War, and Navy building across the Potomac to the military's home grounds. The hearings were conducted at the Pentagon. Instead of sitting as judge, the Budget Bureau examiner shared the responsibility with a Defense Department official. There was a joint review. Recommendations went to the superiors of both men. Most important, the military budget was sub-

mitted to the President by the Secretary of Defense and not
by the Director of the Budget. If there were differences of
opinion, the Budget Director made the appeal. Throughout,
the Defense Department had the upper hand. It sat in a
privileged position. It called the shots.

These practices manifest the power of the military departments and the special privileges accorded them. Deputy
Budget Director Hughes admitted, in testimony to the
House, that what really matters is "sheer power, where the
muscle is. This is a very power-conscious town. The Defense
Establishment is a different group, whether the Congress is
dealing with them or the Budget Bureau, than Head Start."

When new Budget Director Mayo took office early in 1969,
I confronted him, first, with the fact that there were proportionately far too few budget examiners for the big military budget and, second, with the testimony of his predecessors about the hat-in-hand procedures of the Budget Bureau
in deference to the Pentagon. When he returned to testify
in June, Director Mayo said that these procedures had been
changed. The Department of Defense was to be treated like
all other agencies. He emphasized "all."

But, in terms of the number of Budget Bureau analysts assigned to the Department of Defense budget, Mayo confirmed the earlier estimates our Subcommittee had been
given and produced a table indicating that only forty-six
budget analysts were then assigned to review all national
security programs. Later, eight more were added. But, in
view of this paucity of examiners and the pervasive and persistent efforts of the military to avoid close supervision, one
can only wonder what the real difference, if any, over the
next few years will be.

A further flaw in the budget process has been the absence
of "zero base" budgeting. According to Robert Benson, writing in the *Washington Monthly,* "The Defense Department
budgeting process virtually concedes last year's amount and

focuses on whatever incremental changes have been requested. The result, of course, is higher budgets, with past errors compounded year after year." The budget is not reviewed from the ground up. Previous years' items are accepted without evaluation. A critical review is applied only to new proposals. Like old man river, old programs just keep rollin' along.

Similarly, old and reprehensible Pentagon practices continue unchecked and unquestioned. The worst of these is the almost total absence of competition in the award of military contracts.

Traditionally, the government buys by sealed bid. Specifications are written, tenders are sought, bids are received, a public opening takes place, and the contract is awarded to the lowest responsible bidder. Back in the Truman Administration, the President issued an executive order in which seventeen exceptions to the policy of formally advertised competitive bidding for government contracts were made. At that time, President Harry S Truman warned, in severe terms, of the grave danger that the exceptions might become the rule. That danger is here. The exceptions are now the rule. Last year, only 11.5 per cent of all military prime contract awards were let by formally advertised methods. The result is a heavy concentration of defense business in a handful of giant corporations. The practice increases their stranglehold on one of the largest sectors of the economy.

When Secretary Robert S. McNamara took over the helm of the Pentagon, a strenuous attempt was made to improve this practice. Finally, by 1965, the proportion of formally advertised contracts was increased to 17.6 per cent. Figures were produced to show that a shift from a negotiated to a fully competitive contract saved 25 cents on every dollar awarded. Even a shift from a wholly negotiated to a partially competitive contract brought savings of 10 cents on the dollar. Despite McNamara's heroic efforts, however, the old policies prevailed. The proportions slipped from the high water mark of 17.6 per cent in 1965 to 14, then 12, and, finally, 11.5 per cent. Taken by itself, this reduction of formally advertised military contracts from an already low level is evidence of a disgraceful neglect of proper procedures at the Pentagon. But even more revealing of the course of events is the nature of the exceptions.·

Contracts let as exceptions to formal bidding in the category called "Purchases To Keep Facilities Available in the Interest of National Defense or Industrial Mobilization" recently have risen at a fantastic rate. In 1965, only $337 million, or 1.2 per cent, of all prime contracts were let under this authority. By fiscal year 1968, the figure had grown to $4.6 billion, or 11 per cent of the total. The Air Force appeared to be the worst offender among the services. Only 3 per cent of its $12 billion annual expenditure for planes, guns, and missiles was made under formally advertised conditions.

Combined with negotiated and sole source contracts, there is another practice that shelters defense industries from competition and, in fact, guarantees higher costs. This is the inexcusable Pentagon procedure of basing profits on costs rather than as a return of invested capital. Everywhere else, it is standard procedure to measure profits as a return on investment. When profits are based on cost, contractors have no incentive to keep costs down. The incentive is to inflate costs. Still another bad practice, and the one on which Admiral Hyman Rickover trained his biggest guns in testimony before the Subcommittee on Economy in Government, is the Pentagon's failure to insist upon uniform accounting standards among military contractors. "The lack of uniform accounting standards," he told our Subcommittee, "is the biggest loophole in government contracting."

One further DOD shortcoming that the Bureau of the Budget should surely challenge is the manner in which very large military surpluses are generated each year. The value of the items in excess and long supply in the military logistics pipeline is $12.7 billion. This is almost 30 per cent of the total value of all supply systems on hand. Although the proportion of excess and surplus items has dropped over the past decade, $12.7 billion is a lot of money. The basic question about it, which goes unasked, is: What kind of supply system do we have when almost a third of the stocks are in excess of requirements? What kind of supply system is it that generates billions in surplus items?

A final budget abuse is one that unfortunately prevails throughout the U.S. Government and results in massive unneeded spending. This is the practice whereby an agency brazenly commits or spends unused funds, authorized and appropriated for it by Congress, during the last months or days of a fiscal year. Since bureaucrats often are promoted not on how much money they can save but on how much they can get and spend, instead of returning money to the Treasury, they feel compelled to obligate it all. The practice is by no means unique to the Pentagon, but since such large sums are involved in military spending, it becomes particularly wasteful here.

In this regard, an examination of DOD prime contract awards by month is an illuminating exercise. The dull figures tell quite a tale. In 1968, for example, the Pentagon awarded $43.7 billion in prime contracts. The average monthly award came to $3.6 billion. But, in June, the last month of the fiscal year, the amount rose to a spectacular $6 billion, which would make an annual rate of $72 billion. In 1966, total prime contract awards came to $38.2 billion a year, or $3.2 billion a month. In June, Pentagon awards amounted to $7.2 billion, or more than twice the average monthly rate and an annual rate of $86 billion.

The practice of obligating unused funds, universal in government, ordinarily is not loudly spoken about, and certainly not admitted as a policy in writing by any civilian agency. Not so with the Air Force. Where spending is concerned, Air Force officials are shameless. The comptroller at Headquarters, Second Air Force, Strategic Air Command (SAC), put it all in writing. On May 26, 1969, a month before the year closed out, he wrote to base comptrollers, saying, "Except for small amounts—this is all the money you can expect to receive this fiscal year." *"This command,"* he continued, *"will consider the inability to utilize all available resources, whether through document errors or failure to expense all funds, as mismanagement of your financial program."*

The sentence was underlined, possibly as a unique definition of fiscal responsibility.

The efficient headquarters comptroller also ordered base comptrollers to develop and maintain an up-to-date listing of unfunded requirements. *"This is necessary,"* he wrote, and again underlined, *"to insure the immediate expensing of additional funds in the event they may become available during the closing days of the fiscal year."*

He set up a "Funds Command Post" to carry out his orders and called for weekly reports on eleven spending categories during June from base comptrollers. Attached to his letter, insisting that all funds be expended, was an ironic enclosure. It was a copy of President Nixon's Memorandum to the Director of the Bureau of the Budget, which called for "decisive and substantive action to reduce the size of the budget and to keep Federal spending under strict control," and said, "Fiscal responsibility does not come easily. We have a duty, however, to show the way to the Congress and the people. I am confident we can obtain their support."

That, in my opinion, added insult to injury by seeming to suggest that the Director of the Bureau of the Budget should institute an annual award for fiscal subordinates who talk out of both sides of their mouths.

The practice of massive end-of-the-year spending is reprehensible, whether done by the Pentagon or a division of the National Institutes of Health. But in the case of huge prime contracts, the ultimate spending effects proceed in geometrical rather than simple arithmetical progression. A few millions trigger billions. A dollar wasted now often means ten dollars more spent later. It is a quantum jump, a massive release of fiscal energy, a procurement nuclear bomb.

The President's chief fiscal officer, the Director of the Bureau of the Budget, should, of course, ask questions about heavy spending in June, and all the other questions about cost effectiveness, overstocking of surplus items, negotiated contracts, lack of uniform accounting, low bids, or last year's programs. But he should also ask more fundamental questions. Some of them I have already raised in these pages:

Why, in an age of sophisticated missiles, do we need a new manned strategic bomber? Why should we deploy, in the center of Europe, a new main battle tank whose primary strategic purpose is to operate in a tactical nuclear or germ-warfare environment? What cause is served by adding a fifteenth attack carrier in a world where carriers are sitting ducks for modern missiles?

These are the fundamental issues. In this area, the Budget Bureau has struck out. A single example, the continental air defense system, illustrates the Bureau's failure. It is one of many examples that could serve this purpose.

The United States has spent some $18 billion to deploy what is known as the SAGE continental air defense system. In fiscal year, 1970, the Pentagon proposed additional billions for the AWACS system to improve and supersede SAGE. But what is this air defense system for? It was first authorized against a possible Russian threat. Its purpose was to deter a Russian intercontinental bomber strike, even though the Russians, at the time, had no effective intercontinental bomber force. Over several years, the threat did not materialize, but the funds for SAGE were spent, nevertheless.

The Pentagon argued for SAGE on ever more spurious grounds. First, officials said that it was needed to keep the Russians from reversing their decision and going ahead to build a new intercontinental bomber. That is, they argued that it was necessary to build a defense against a nonexistent threat to prevent emergence of a threat. Second, they said the continental air defense system was to guard against Russian medium-range bombers. Since these bombers were unable to fly from the Soviet Union to the United States with a full bomb load and return, what the Pentagon planners were arguing here was that we had to deploy SAGE, and now must deploy AWACS, to guard against a one-way, Russian-*kamikaze* attack.

Critics pointed out that this was an absurd argument because our basic security against any attack from the Soviet Union is our missile deterrent. We already possess an ability to destroy the Russians altogether, if they launch a war, whether by high-speed missile or slow-moving, suicidal medium bombers. Senator John Sherman Cooper, in a moving speech just before the crucial Senate ABM vote, described this deterrent well:

> We have a kind of security today. It is the ability to destroy the Soviet Union or any other power. The Soviet Union has this security as well.
>
> The pursuit of security through nuclear power alone will never end. It will waste the fruits of the earth and make the labor of men empty. It will increase the sense of futility, particularly among the young. For we and the Soviet, with all our technology, can be reduced to dust at any moment. The green earth and millions who live on it can be burned to gray ashes. This specter is the essence of the nuclear arms race. This is our present security.

The proponents of SAGE and AWACS have shifted ground again and now claim that we need AWACS to protect those missiles that we would hold in reserve following any retaliatory or second strike we might launch after being hit by an enemy. But the fact is that SAGE and AWACS are billion-dollar boondoggles predicated on a nonexistent Soviet bomber threat. No one has exposed their absurdity more clearly than former Budget Director Charles Schultze, in a brilliant *tour de force* before our Subcommittee in June, 1969.

Yet, when Schultze was asked why the system was ever approved if it was so clearly unneeded, he answered bluntly and truthfully, in a burst of candor unprecedented in Washington political circles, that no one had raised that fundamental question. No one had asked, "Why do we need it?"

The process by which the Budget Bureau approves the military budget is loaded against the taxpayer. The results weaken our security and threaten our national well-being. Several important alternatives to spending $18 billion on SAGE and AWACS existed. We could have financed, probably at a much lower cost, a different kind of weapon system, genuinely necessary for the security of the United States. We could have spent funds for housing, jobs, or schools, which, over a period of time, would provide a multifold return on the dollars expended. Finally, all or a portion of the $18 billion might have been returned to the taxpayers in the form of a smaller tax burden.

In fact, if the Budget Bureau—and Congress—had given the $18 billion spent on SAGE the same detailed study they gave the $12 billion surtax and its extension, the surtax would never have been needed.

There are other institutional failures, too. Congress, as we shall see in the next chapter, is also guilty. But one other Presidential agency, in addition to the Bureau of the Budget, must bear a portion of the blame for our present state of affairs, in which the military budget is out of control.

The President's Council of Economic Advisers, like the

Bureau of the Budget, has abdicated its responsibilities for defense spending. Its present Chairman, Paul McCracken, testified before our Subcommittee that "the Council is not a good source of information on the national security consequences of alternative national defense strategies and programs." But if it is not, who is? And what of the Council's surveillance of the consequences of defense spending on the national economy?

The military budget uses 8 to 10 per cent of the gross national product. It comprises 80 per cent of the controllable items in the entire national budget. Its economic impact is greater than that of any other single expenditure. It has massive effects on our balance of payments. It impinges on local labor markets. It can bid up the price of key commodities. Its inflationary effects are more severe than those of most other types of expenditures. It affects both the human and natural resources available for other high priorities; one-tenth of the nation's scientists and one-fifth of its engineers are employed directly on national defense work. Its ramifications and permutations affect the economy at every juncture.

Yet, as this book is written, the President's Council of Economic Advisers has yet to make a thorough analysis of the DOD budget. It has concerned itself only with that budget's general numbers. It has made few studies distinguishing between the economic impact of a defense dollar and that spent for another government function or expended privately. It has done no studies on the regional impacts of defense spending, although that spending is concentrated in a few states and a relatively few companies. With respect to the military budget, it has limited its role to what the economists call macroeconomics, which means that it has taken no more than a general and uncritical look at the broad effects of defense expenditures.

It has made no study of how defense spending affects manpower and the demand for manpower, no study of the enormous rise in defense prices over the last four years, and no study of the economic effects of the present loose practices of military procurement in order to eliminate the huge economic inefficiencies that flow from these practices.

When Admiral Rickover testified about the Pentagon's "weighted guidelines" system of profit determination for the Joint Economic Committee's Subcommittee on Economy in Government, he said that under the system the profits on defense contracts have increased by about 25 per cent without regard to contractor performance. The feisty Admiral also charged that defense contractors are asking higher and higher profits. Large contractors are reporting record profits to their stockholders, he said. He cited chapter and verse:

1. Suppliers of propulsion turbines are insisting on 20 to 25 per cent profit, as compared with 10 per cent a few years ago.
2. Several nuclear equipment suppliers are requesting 15 to 20 per cent profit.
3. Profit percentages on shipbuilding contracts have doubled in the past two years.
4. One division of a large company recently priced equipment to a Navy shipbuilder at a 33 per cent profit.

The Admiral asserted that these examples were only a few of the number he had seen in the course of his recent work for the Navy's Nuclear Propulsion Program. He charged that, while wholesale prices of manufactured goods had risen about 15 per cent since 1959, prices for military equipment had gone up 30, 40, 50 per cent, and more.

That the committee of Congress with explicit jurisdiction over the question of prices, profits, and production was unable to get such data from the Council of Economic Advisers, or from the departments of Commerce or Labor, but had to turn to Admiral Rickover for the information is, in itself, a reflection on the inadequacy of the supervision over the military budget.

The economic consequences of the military budget are no-where properly assessed. This failure by the Council of Economic Advisers is one of the reasons the country has lost control over military spending.

There is, in fact, no institution in the executive branch of the government that is now geared to make a critical and analytical review of the military budget. This is true with respect to the economic consequences of particular defense procurements decisions, such as their effects on prices, wages and output. It is true, today, with respect to whether a particular authorized weapon is really needed. It is also true with respect to budgetary alternatives. No one calculates or decides whether $2 billion is better spent on subsidizing three-and-a-third million low-income housing units for a full year or on the overrun on the C-5A airplane. In no part of the Executive Office of the President are such questions asked, such issues focused, and such decisions made, even though merely to ask the obvious questions is often to answer them. The right questions have not been asked.

Characteristically, Admiral Rickover concluded his testimony before our Subcommittee with a fighting statement. The issue, he observed, is "who is going to be in control, the government or industry?"

He also warned that "the Congress must constantly bear in mind the growing autonomy of the federal bureaucracy, the increasing lack of control by the Congress, and the bureaucratic tendency to make accommodations with industrial corporations."

"If a close partnership between government and industry is actually necessary," he observed, "then a great responsibility rests on the Congress and on the executive branch to see to it that these giant organizations do not become, in effect, a fourth branch of government—a fourth branch, but with men exerting power without political or legal responsibility."

Why has this responsibility not been properly discharged? Why is it true that the Budget Bureau spends at least four times the man-hours on a dollar for the poverty program that it does on a military item? Why, until this year, has Congress debated a $2 to $3 billion foreign-aid bill for days when it shouted through the gigantic defense budget in minutes? How does $18 billion for SAGE and AWACS slip through Congress without debate while the central cities of the United States are starved for funds?

One reason for the failure both of executive agencies and Congress is the sheer size of the military budget. It is almost impossible for any man or agency or arm of government to comprehend, let alone control, $80 billion in funds.

In addition, there is the political atmosphere in which military budgets have been determined. On this point, former Budget Director Schultze testified before the Economy in Government Subcommittee:

> Primarily we have large military budgets because the American people, in the Cold War environment of the nineteen fifties and sixties, have pretty much been willing to buy anything carrying the label "Needed for National Security." The political climate has, until recently, been such that on fundamental matters, it was exceedingly difficult to challenge military judgments, and still avoid the stigma of playing fast and loose with national security.

At bottom, we have the Soviet Union to thank. After World War II, the Red Army remained in the center of Europe. Greece and Turkey were threatened. Berlin was blockaded. Czechoslovakia was taken over. Hungary was seized. The Russian threat was real, not imagined. We responded where we could, properly. Europe was saved and World War III has thus far been averted.

But, apart from the world political atmosphere, there are many other reasons why we have reached the present state.

As Schultze, now an economist at the University of Maryland and the Brookings Institution, described it before the Economy in Government Subcommittee's hearings entitled "National Priorities and the Military Budget," a myriad of forces have continued to promote escalation of military costs. He described four of them in detail.

First, there is the impact of modern technology on the strategic nuclear forces, best illustrated by the advent of the MIRV's and ABM's.

The goal of American military planners had been to preserve what is called an "assured destructive capacity," which is nothing more than the ability to strike back at an enemy so audacious as to strike first. With over 1,000 intercontinental missiles, 41 submarines armed with Polaris and Poseidon missiles, 650 intercontinental bombers, plus bases and aircraft carriers from which planes can fly and medium-range missiles can be lofted into the skies, we have the capacity to absorb a "first strike," recover, and deliver a devastating blow to any enemy so foolish as to launch such an attack.

One of the advantages both sides in the prolonged Cold War have held, which has added to the "stability" of the strategic situation, is the cost advantage to the defender. Because of the inaccuracies of the intercontinental missiles, at least two of them have been needed to knock out one hardened missile site. Thus, a potential aggressor, in order to assure a first-strike capability—the ability to knock out the other country's retaliatory force—has needed at least two missiles in his armory for every one of the defender. This ratio has made it possible for a nation to preserve its retaliatory force at roughly half the cost to the nation seeking a first-strike capability. Much of what is known as "mutual deterrence" has been based on this economic fact.

With the development of the multiple, independently targeted, re-entry vehicle (MIRV), this situation has changed. One missile can now fire several warheads. The advantage to the defender is greatly decreased. Furthermore, the new guidance systems can be highly accurate. What intellectual arguments there are for the ABM are based on these facts.

The result is another quantum jump in costs. More missiles and warheads, new, highly sophisticated guidance systems, and "defensive" anti-ballistic-missile deployment add billions to the cost of providing an "assured destructive capacity."

That is point number one. Each side must run faster to stay even.

In addition, Schultze said, "A second major factor in driving arms budgets up is the propensity of military planners to prepare against almost every conceivable contingency or risk." He cited the SAGE-AWACS example and the F-14 Navy aircraft, whose basic purpose was to defend the fleet against a Soviet supersonic bomber and missile threat, as cases in point. (Another critic of the F-14, Chairman George H. Mahon of the House Appropriations Committee, has tartly observed, "The bomber threat against the fleet, as you know, has been predicted by Navy officials for some time. It has not, of course, developed to date.")"It is my judgment," Schultze said, "that we generally have tended in the postwar period to tip the balance too strongly in favor of spending large sums in attempting to cover a wide range of remote contingencies."

Summing up his first two points, he continued, "This tendency—combined with the relentless ability of modern technology to create new contingencies and new systems to combat them—threatens to produce sizeable increases in the defense budget."

A third important tendency, cited by Schultze as a major cause of the escalation of military costs, was what Malcolm Hoag has called "modernization inflation." Simply put, this means no more than that planes with greater speed, range, bombloads, accuracy of fire, loiter time, and ability to locate targets cost a great deal more money. Similarly, with carriers, missiles, and weapons, as Schultze testified, "We pay sharply increased costs to obtain sharply increased performance." The flaw, he pointed out, is that "seldom if ever, is this advance in 'quality' used to justify a reduction in the *number* of planes or carriers or destroyers or tanks." This point is especially telling in instances where the Russians have no comparable weapon, as is the case with carriers or attack bombers.

Finally, former Budget Director Schultze testified, perhaps the most important factor in increasing military budgets is that "some of the most fundamental decisions which determine the size of these budgets are seldom subjected to outside review and only occasionally discussed and debated in the arena."

Like Topsy, many of the United States' basic decisions "just grew." This is true of our two-and-one-half war policy. It is true of our commitment to help defend some forty-odd nations in the world. Few people could cite the treaty or commitment under which we have pledged our resources to friendly, neutral, and even semi-hostile nations. Many of them are old, made in different economic circumstances, and under very different strategic considerations.

The Senate Foreign Relations Committee's Subcommittee on U.S. Security Agreements and Commitments Abroad recently has been examining many of these commitments in secret hearings. The National Security Council has been engaged in a similar study. They also should be publicly reviewed.

We need to take a new look at even the most successful of our policies, such as those toward Western Europe, made shortly after World War II when European nations were in dire economic need. With the Red Army on its frontiers, Western Europe was incapable of feeding itself, let alone defending itself. How different all that is now. Yet many of the policies made in those dark days continue. The United States is called on to make a disproportionate effort in the defense of Europe, in the support of Free World trade policies, and in aid to less fortunate nations. No country in Europe has met its military commitments to NATO. Few of them have supported the underdeveloped and emerging nations with the volume of aid they are capable of giving in view of their prosperous economies and vastly diminished military and defense commitments.

In addition, the United States and Great Britain have borne great burdens as the "key currency" nations of the world, while much of Europe has retained restrictive trade barriers long after the reasons justifying them have vanished.

In these circumstances, is it our responsibility to be able to fight *simultaneously* a NATO war, a major war in Asia such as a Red Chinese attack on Southeast Asia, and a minor *contretemps* such as that which occurred in the Dominican Republic? That has been the policy on the basis of which our military forces are planned and deployed. Why were the fundamental questions about it, which the public is now asking, not raised earlier by our institutions of government?

The genuine justifications for the escalation of the military budget have produced an inverse response. As the need to review the defense budget increased, the critical efforts diminished. For too long, none of the institutions designed to check military spending have actually functioned. The Pentagon itself has too many conflicting self-interests within it to act as critic and umpire over its own destiny. The Budget Bureau and the Council of Economic Advisers abandoned the task. Congress has been a pushover for the Pentagon. The teeth of the General Accounting Office, watchdog for the legislative branch over Pentagon spending, were pulled by highly placed congressional members of the military-industrial complex.

When the executive and legislative branches of the government abandoned the budgetary field, the military hierarchy rushed into the vacuum. A series of practices and rationalizations grew up that protected and re-enforced the Pentagon's position and power.

A Congressional staffer once likened the present situation to a sign he had seen in a rural restaurant: "Southern Hungarian goulash baked kosher style." It includes the special status accorded the military by the Budget Bureau, the absence of examination by the Council of Economic Advisers, the unjustified proportion of negotiated contracts, the special means of calculating profits, the lack of a uniform accounting system, the huge excesses and surpluses in supplies, the military propensity to demand annual weapons improvements and to meet every actual risk as well as several that do not exist at all, and the tendency of some in Congress to give the Department of Defense *carte blanche*.

This whole network of Pentagon privilege will have to be unraveled if we are to regain control of the defense budget. There is a great deal of work to be done, a great many searching questions to be asked, both on Capitol Hill and, across the city, in the high-ceiling rooms of the venerated Executive Office Building.

V

Congress: Pushover
for the Pentagon

ON JULY 3, 1969, S. 2546, a bill "to authorize appropriations during the fiscal year 1970 for procurement of aircraft, missiles, naval vessels, and tracked combat vehicles, and research, development, test, and evaluation for the Armed Forces" was reported to the Senate under the authority of the order of the previous day.

The short 5-page bill was 116 lines long. It contained only 888 words. But it authorized a grand total of twenty billion, fifty-nine million, five hundred thousand dollars for missiles, planes, tanks and ships. This was $4 billion a page and almost $22.6 million a word.

In years gone by, this proposed legislation would have been shouted through in far fewer minutes than its 888 words. But 1969 was different. For the first time, a major military authorization bill was under attack. The bill would not finally pass until September 18, or eleven weeks after it became the business of the Senate.

Meanwhile, the funds it contained for ABM deployment squeaked through when a 51-49 vote defeated the Cooper-Hart amendment to prevent deployment. The Senate adopted amendments reducing research and development funds. It voted unanimously to restrict chemical and biological warfare funds and operations. Conditions were attached to contracts for major weapons. With the ABM as the central issue, the Senate, for the first time in two decades, challenged major weapons systems themselves—the missiles, planes, tanks, and ships that must be authorized annually. Later, the appropriation bill, which provides the actual funds for the manpower, administration, and procurement in fiscal year 1970, came under serious attack. Over $8 billion was pared from the original request.

The Senate had seen nothing like this for decades. Less than a handful of senators had even been in office when such a critical review had last taken place.

For years, Congress had been a pushover for the Pentagon. It had gone along with the military's wishes, and a protective network of practices and traditions had grown up around the military procurement and appropriations bills, the members of the Armed Services and Appropriations committees who handle them, and the relationship of the Pentagon to members of both houses of Congress.

The Armed Services and Appropriations Committees are among the most powerful in the House and Senate. The power they exercise can be compared only with that of the House Ways and Means Committee, which is the Democratic "committee on committees" in the House and which gains strength from the Constitutional provision that all revenue bills shall originate in the House.

Consequently, as sugar attracts bees, those members of

both houses who tend to be more interested in political
power than in issues or the substance of legislation swarm to
the Armed Services and Appropriations Committees. Their
composition is more conservative than most other committees
or their parent bodies. Their members are more senior than
those found on other committees, in an institution where
seniority itself is looked upon as the greatest virtue. It is
also true that, man for man, they are among the ablest members of Congress. The abilities of Senator Richard B. Russell,
of Georgia, and John Stennis, of Mississippi, are unsurpassed
in the Senate. Men like Stuart Symington, of Missouri, and
Henry M. Jackson, of Washington, and the Senate's gentle
lady, Margaret Chase Smith, of Maine, have unequaled repu-
tations among their colleagues for intelligence, industry, and
patriotism. Not only do members of these committees excel
in power and seniority, but man for man (and woman for
woman) they have as much brain power and natural ability
as can be found among the leaders in any walk of American
life. On the whole, the country is lucky to have them at the
seats of power. They are devoted human beings, who suffer
more political slings and arrows than should be inflicted on
them. They exercise a profound and deeply ethical judgment
over the affairs of men. In many respects, they deserve better
from fellow citizens than the public criticism they get.

The committees on which they serve are, however, dominated by sectionalism. In the Senate, five of the six top
Democratic members on the Appropriations Committee are
from south of the Mason-Dixon line. In the House, six of
the top eight Democratic members of the Appropriations
Committee came from Dixieland. On the Armed Services
committees, four of six top Democrats in the Senate and
three of five in the House are from the South.

Among Republicans, conservative Midwestern members
clearly dominate the top positions on both House and Senate
Appropriations committees. They hold three of the four

highest positions in the Senate and six of the top ten in the House. Republican Armed Services Committee membership follows no distinctive regional pattern. But five out of eight of its Senate members are clearly among the most conservative in the Senate, namely Strom Thurmond, of South Carolina, John Tower, of Texas, Peter Dominick, of Colorado, George Murphy, of California, and Barry Goldwater, of Arizona.

The regional cast of the committees is seen most clearly in the home districts and states of their chairmen. For years, in both House and Senate the chairmen of the Armed Service committees were from the state of Georgia. Richard Brevard Russell, the Senate's Dean and President Pro Tempore, chaired the Senate Armed Services Committee. Now he heads the even more powerful Senate Appropriations Committee. His place on Armed Services has been taken by the courtly and highly respected John Stennis, of Mississippi.

In the period when Representative Carl Vinson, of Georgia, Senator Russell's counterpart, held sway as Chairman of the House Armed Services Committee, one of the apocryphal Washington stories dealt with the seeming ease by which military installations were located in Georgia. At the suggestion that a New Air Force base be placed in the "Peach" state, it is reported that one very brave Air Force general said, "One more base would sink it."

The power that these committee chairmen exercise is formidable indeed. At times, however, it may be exaggerated. There is no real way to judge it. For example, it was while Senator Russell was Chairman of the Senate Armed Services Committee that the huge C-5A contract went to Lockheed's Marietta, Georgia, plant. Boeing, located in the states of Washington and Kansas, was the original choice of the Air Force Contract Selection Board, but the prize went to Lockheed after higher-ups changed the award when Lockheed's bid was $300 million lower than Boeing's, and $100 million below the third competitor, McDonnell Douglas, of St. Louis.

Many give Senator Russell credit for landing the contract. Others differ.

There are public reports that Senator Russell himself was originally lukewarm about the project because some in the Air Force argued that the need for the plane was limited, since existing air and ship cargo capacity was efficient and sufficient for any contingency. Senator Russell's feelings stemmed not so much from that point, however, as from another. He believed that the planes might in a day or two get us into a war that would take years to get out of. He feared that a deployment capability could overextend our commitments.

Some Lockheed Company spokesmen believe that the influence of such men as Senator Russell and Congressman Vinson is overrated. "At best," one Lockheed executive was quoted as saying about the congressional delegation, "they hold the line and prevent you from being manipulated out of a contract you deserve." He went on to say that it was Lockheed's experience in designing cargo planes and its past performance on military contracting that was the key to the contract. He claimed that these factors were far more important than the influence of either Senator Russell, Congressman Vinson, or other members of the Georgia delegation.

However, that view, although it may be the correct one, is not shared by the mayor of Marietta, Georgia, Howard Atherton. Mayor Atherton believes that Senator Russell was the key to landing the contract for which, at the crucial stage, Atherton sought the senior Senator's help, according to a series of articles on defense spending by Patrick Sloyan, of the Hearst News Bureau in Washington. Lockheed, Marietta's largest employer, was at the end of its contract for the C-141 Starlifter, which was then the world's largest cargo plane. "Without the new contract, Lockheed told us that for a start they would lay off 10,000 workers. So we started to work," Sloyan quoted Atherton as saying. The mayor took his case to Senator Russell in Washington.

"The trouble was that Russell didn't think the C-5A was really needed," Atherton is reported to have said. Apparently, Air Force internal studies agreed with that view. There would be an excess amount of air cargo capacity for some time to come. "The Starlifter can carry anything the C-5A can except a missile or some really big piece of Army gear. It was just a case that one C-5A could do the work of a couple of planes you already had flying," Atherton told Sloyan.

In addition, Atherton said that the Senator believed that Secretary McNamara was going ahead with the C-5A in order to "give the plane to Boeing because Boeing got left out on the TFX fighter." Senator Russell, nevertheless, took the case to the White House. According to Mayor Atherton, "He talked to President Johnson about it. Without Russell, we wouldn't have gotten the contract."

In their private conversations, many Air Force officials speculate that the crucial issue in the C-5A case was maintaining Lockheed as a defense contractor. Certainly, critics of defense contracting believe that which one of the modern aerospace companies, now almost wholly dependent on defense contracts, needs the business is the single most important consideration in choosing a contractor. It far exceeds in importance the matters of cost, quality, or delivery date, which are the ostensible reasons for granting awards to particular companies.

On March 2, 1968, the roll-out ceremony for the football-field-sized C-5A took place at Marietta. President Lyndon B. Johnson was the featured speaker. He sang the praises of his old Senate comrade and closest political ally in the Senate in these words:

> I would have you good folks of Georgia to know that there are a lot of Marietta, Georgias, scattered throughout our fifty States.
>
> All of them would like to have the pride that comes

from this production. But not all of them have the Georgia delegation.

The President then went on to refer again to Senator Russell and Congressman Vinson in glowing terms.

In any event, it can surely be said that the chairmanships of the House and Senate Armed Services Committees held by Senator Russell and Congressman Vinson did not hurt Georgia. Primarily because of Lockheed, Georgia ranks second in the net value of prime military contracts received for airframes and related assemblies and spares with 12.1 per cent of the national total.

But it can also be said that Senator Russell and the new Chairman of the Senate Armed Services Committee, John Stennis, apply a sophisticated and, at times, critical attitude toward local pressures and Pentagon requests. Representative L. Mendel Rivers, of South Carolina, the successor to Congressman Vinson as Chairman of the House Armed Services Committee, has no such inhibitions.

Rivers' nine-county First District in South Carolina, which centers on Charleston, has been described as a "microcosm of the miltary-industrial complex." Among its numerous Army, Navy, Air Force, and Marine Corps installations are the Charleston Air Force Base, the Charleston Army Depot, the Charleston Navy Shipyard, the Marine Corps Air Station at Beaufort, the famous Marine Corps Recruit Depot at Parris Island, the Naval Hospital at Charleston, the Naval Hospital at Beaufort, the Naval Station at Charleston, and the Naval Supply Center, the Naval Weapons Station, the Navy Fleet Ballistic Missile Submarine Training Center, and the Navy's Polaris Missile Facility, all also at Charleston.

There is an old saying that Charleston, South Carolina, is where the Ashley and Cooper rivers join to form the Atlantic Ocean. Now it is claimed that Charleston is the confluence of the Ashley, Cooper, and Mendel Rivers, which converge there to form the world's second largest salt water body. The Congressman's campaign slogan is "Rivers Delivers." The military services and sundry administrative bureaucrats, aware of the power he flexes on Capitol Hill, have named the main entrance to the Charleston Air Force Base "Rivers Gate," although it is a rule that federal installations are never named for officials during their lifetime. Highway route number 52 through the city is called "Rivers Avenue," and a housing project on the Navy Base is called "Men-Riv Park."

The Congressman makes no bones about his influence. He claims to have brought in 90 per cent of these Charleston installations during the nearly thirty years since he was elected to the Seventy-seventh Congress on November 5, 1940. Fully aware of the perquisites of the position he holds and with no qualms about exercising them, he once told a colleague, "I could defeat Strom Thurmond any day in the week. But I don't want to be a South Carolina Senator. I've got the most powerful position in the U.S. Congress."

When the military procurement authorization bill was in the House, Congressman Rivers successfully pushed through a bill that was $1.5 billion higher than the Senate's $20 billion. One billion of this amount was in new shipbuilding authorizations, which Rivers demanded even though the Pentagon did not want it. Another $28 million was included for Rivers's pet project, the Freedom Fighter, for which there is no U.S. defense requirement. After beating down floor amendments to cut weapons-systems funds or to make other changes in procurement practices, the South Carolina Congressman told both press and television that his legislative success exceeded anything recorded by "Julius Caesar in all his glory." He vowed that he would never "surrender my toga."

Given the power of committee chairmen in the House, the almost $80 billion budget he authorized, and his propensity, unlike his Senate opposite numbers, to throw his weight around, the Congressman's description of himself may well be true. Chairmen of Senate committees exercise their power largely through strength of personality and character. On the whole, they command respect by example, not authority. In the House, committee chairmen have far more formidable and autocratic power. Congressman Rivers runs his forty-man committee with an iron hand. He retains control over the appointments to subcommittees. As a result, the two or three high-spirited souls on his committee find they are members of only two, instead of three or four subcommittees.

Rivers once introduced one of his committee members, Charles W. Whalen, Jr., of Ohio, as the "representative from Wright-Patterson Air Force Base." Whalen had aroused the Chairman's ire by raising questions over the C-5A overruns.

Members' time for questioning witnesses is limited to five minutes each, by a series of alarm clocks perched at the Chairman's seat. Hearings often end on Thursdays. Minority or dissenting views are due Friday morning. The House Rules Committee grants a closed rule (no floor amendments) on Monday, and the bill comes up Tuesday. This has been the no-nonsense way the huge military authorization bills pass the House.

One member told Warren Unna, of the *Washington Post,* that the House Armed Services Committee is the only committee that asks the executive agency it oversees, in this case the Pentagon, "Do you have enough?" instead of "Do you really have to have it?" Sometimes, as in the case of Chairman Rivers's extra $1 billion for ship construction, the approach seems to be "Take this whether or not you need it."

In the spring of 1969, a mild but courageous critic of the Pentagon and the C-5A contract, Representative William Moorhead, of Pennsylvania, appeared on Walter Cronkite's TV evening news and criticized the close relationships between defense contractors and some members of Congress, without naming names. He brought down Mendel Rivers's wrath upon his head.

Congressman Moorhead had said only that he thought some members of Congress "have dealt so long with the military and with the defense contractors that they begin to think they are without fault and obviously people do make mistakes." But Congressman Rivers apparently took fellow member Moorhead's general observations as a personal criticism. He whipped off the following letter to the Pennsylvanian:

Dear Mr. Moorhead:

Last night I listened to the Walter Cronkite program on television.

Among other things I gained the impression from comments that you feel members of Congress who historically have dealt with military procurement have in substance become the handmaidens of the Department of Defense and defense contractors.

I am sure you realize that this is a very serious charge because each of us including yourself took the same oath as members of Congress.

I also consider this implied condemnation as personally directed at me as chairman of the House Armed Services Committee and at each member of the committee.

Under the circumstances, I have no alternative but to invite you to appear before the committee to present whatever evidence you may have to substantiate your allegations.

We are in the midst of considering the military procurement authorization bill. Therefore I hope you will tell me what early date would be convenient for you to appear before the committee.

Sincerely,
MENDEL RIVERS

Moorhead replied to this command invitation that he would be honored to appear, but after it became public, Chairman Rivers withdrew his request.

The South Carolina Congressman deals with not only his own committee members but also soft-spoken critics like Congressman Moorhead, in an arbitrary and astringent fash ion. He does the same with fellow chairmen, even one as important and powerful as Congressman George H. Mahon, of Texas, the Chairman of the House Appropriations Com- mittee and the fourth member of the Southern quadrum- virate, which heads the Appropriations and Armed Services committees in Congress.

George H. Mahon came to Congress in 1934. Thirty years later, in 1964, he became Chairman of the House Appropria- tions Committee. Meanwhile, he collected a half dozen honorary degrees and the American Political Science As- sociation's Congressional Distinguished Service Award. Al- though never a serious Pentagon critic, he is known as a quiet, conservative, conscientious, and hard-working member of Congress. Like John Stennis in the Senate, he is one of dozens of congressmen who receive little publicity but serve the country well. The APSA Award is a tribute to his dis- tinguished effort.

His Texas Panhandle district is not weighted down with Army bases or Air Force runways, although Texas has been the recipient of vast military and space contracts, which have moved it from ninth to second place among the states in lists of contracts received since the fourth quarter of 1964.

In the course of supporting a supplemental appropriations bill, which contained a fiscal year 1970 spending ceiling of a whopping $192.9 billion, Chairman Mahon charged that "The military has made so many mistakes, it has generated a lack of confidence." The powerful Texan, who also heads the Defense Appropriations Subcommittee of his full committee, cited as proof the sinking of the $50 million submarine *Guittaro,* while under construction at the Mare Island Naval Shipyard in California's San Francisco Bay. Chairman Ma-

hon charged that the Navy would probably transfer and promote the officer in charge rather than punish him with a
court-martial.

Obviously irritated by the Texan's remarks, Congressman
Rivers stormed to the well of the House, where he grabbed
a microphone and shouted, "This is the way to tear down the
military! That is one of the most popular things you could
say. Keep on saying it, and the enemies of the military will
love you for saying it!"

As for the enemies of the military, Chairman Rivers asserted that "the other body (the Senate) is full of them."

Earlier, Rivers had responded to Mahon's general remarks
by complaining, "Whenever we look for reductions, everybody looks to the military. This Congress hasn't got the guts
to get out here and stop some of the crazy programs we've
got."

The Armed Services Chairman then cited the Job Corps
as his choice example of a "crazy" program. Job Corps funds
amount to about $280 million a year, or about one-three
hundredth the amount spent on the military and space programs.

House Appropriations Committee Chairman Mahon observed that even with the fiscal year 1970 ceiling on spending
the Defense Department could spend $80 billion. This was
enough, he averred, "if the military is run properly."

The tendency for military contracts and military bases to
be concentrated in key states and regions led Congressman
Kenneth Hechler, of West Virginia, to kick up a fuss about
it when he first came to the House. Coming as he did from
one of the poorest states, he objected to the pork-barrel aspects of defense spending in the following terms: "I am
firmly against the kind of logrolling which would subject
our defense program to narrowly sectional or selfish pulling
or hauling."

But, he said, "I am getting pretty hot under the collar

about the way my state of West Virginia is shortchanged by the Army, Navy, and Air Force."

During World War II, many servicemen concluded that an overwhelming proportion of military training was at Southern bases because the warm climate made possible year-round operations. When they were assigned to duty in Alaska or fought over Western Europe's snow-laden ground with Patton or Bradley in the winter of 1944–45, their curiosity about why they were trained in the South to fight wars in the cold must been aroused. Climate had little to do with it. Seniority in Congress did.

The military services themselves are among the biggest lobbies in the country. They are especially solicitous of the members of the Armed Services and Appropriations Committees. As the *Congressional Quarterly* reported:

> When a senior member of the House Armed Services Committee complained of rumors that a Marine Corps installation might be removed from his district, the commandant came in person to assure him that no change would be made "so long as I am in the job."
>
> A junior Committee member, on learning that an unsolicited Army training center was to be located in his district, concluded that "someone" in the Pentagon was looking out for his interests.

The Pentagon spends a minimum of $4 million a year on its 339 congressional liaison specialists, the polite term for lobbyists. This is more than one for every two of the 535 members of the House and Senate.

When former Secretary Robert McNamara announced the closing of some 95 military bases in 1964, the *Wall Street Journal* reported that the Secretary received 169 congressional phone calls before the end of the afternoon of the day of the announcement.

Malcolm Moos, now President of the University of Minnesota and the man who drafted President Eisenhower's famous

military-industrial complex speech, attributed part of its
origins to the pressures received from Congress. "I was constantly impressed with the test of wills going on in Congress,"
Moos said, "about taking a military installation away from
this or that state and what it would do to the economy and
the fighting back and forth."

The general indictment that the press, the public, and
members of Congress themselves have made against the Congress as a pushover for the Pentagon has many specific items.

"One hundred of the 435 House members and 39 of the
100 Senators have officer ranks as high as major general,"
William McGaffin and Robert Gruenberg of the *Chicago
Daily News* reported, after digging deep into Pentagon files.

Congressional Quarterly identified some 991 major private
defense plants and defense-oriented government installations
in 363 of the 435 congressional districts. That means that 85
per cent of all members of the House and Senate have major
installations in their states or districts.

Although the Defense Department and the Budget Bureau
must bear a primary share of the responsibility for the fact
that military spending is out of control, the Congress has
also failed in its duty. So far as Congress has been concerned,
military spending has been out of control for many years.

The Constitution clearly states that:

> The Congress shall have Power . . . To raise and support
> Armies . . . To provide and maintain a Navy . . . To make
> Rules for the Government and Regulation of the land and
> naval Forces.

It also provides that no appropriation of money to raise and
support armies shall be for a longer term than two years.

The problem today is whether Congress is willing and
ready to exercise its Constitutional responsibility. This cannot be done by abdicating or delegating authority over mili-

tary budgets and military weapons to the Pentagon. In this sense, Congress has failed to exercise its duty to provide for the common defense.

There is another sense in which Congress has failed. It has not given sufficient attention to the effect of waste in the military budget on other vital nonmilitary national undertakings.

Senator Symington has said, "Too many officials in Washington can hear the sound of the farthest drum before the cry of a single child in the streets." And, in a recent speech, the man who presided over the Senate Armed Services Committee for years and who now chairs the Appropriations Committee, Senator Richard Russell, of Georgia, stated:

> There is something about preparing for destruction that causes men to be more careless in spending money than they would be if they were building for constructive purposes.
>
> What this is, I do not know; but I have observed over a period of almost thirty years in the Senate that there is something about buying arms with which to kill, to destroy, to wipe out cities and to obliterate great transportation systems which causes men not to reckon the dollar cost as closely as they do when they think about proper housing and the care of the health of human beings.

Senator Russell's point is well illustrated by Congressman Rivers's directive to cut the $280 million Job Corps, but touch not a hair on the fair head of the Pentagon's $80 billion.

Congress's traditional role as a profligate military spender and its much more recent role as persistent Pentagon critic are today in conflict. Which will win? If Congress is to heal itself or its debilitating schizophrenia in this regard, it must foster a climate of criticism and meticulously examine every request for weapons and arms.

A good beginning in this vitally necessary self-reform was

made in 1969 when, for the first time in over two decades, the military citadel was charged.

In the Senate, the ABM system was challenged. The Joint Economic Committee held its subcommittee hearings on the C-5A, other weapon-system overruns, the Russian economic potential, and economic priorities and the military budget.

The Peace-Through-Law group headed by Senator Mark Hatfield, of Oregon, addressed itself to other weapons systems. Altogether, $3 billion was cut from President Johnson's original $23 billion request for the procurement of new tanks, planes, guns, ships, and missiles, and for research. One billion of this was cut when, in the new critical climate, President Nixon reviewed the Johnson budget. Part of another billion was saved when, under pressure to cut spending, the Defense Department abandoned the Manned Orbiting Laboratory (MOL) and canceled the Cheyenne helicopter project. In the climate of the past, these wasteful and inefficient projects would have continued.

The Armed Services Committee, for the first time in modern history, organized to make a more critical examination of the military requests. Subcommittees were set up. Far more penetrating hearings were held on the ABM, on research and development, and on requests for funds for tanks, carriers, planes, and ships than ever before. And the committee itself cut almost a billion from the original requests for research and development and such items as the Fast Deployment Logistic Ships.

The new climate also affected debate on the Senate floor. Six weeks were spent on the ABM, and while that fight ended in a technical loss but a moral victory, others were won outright.

The proposal by Senator Richard Schweiker, of Pennsylvania, for quarterly reports on weapons-systems cost status, won passage by a single vote over the vehement objections of the Pentagon supporters.

A series of amendments to impose strict limits on production of weapons for chemical and biological warfare, drafted by Senator Gaylord Nelson, of Wisconsin, Senator Hatfield, and an *ad hoc* bipartisan group, passed unanimously.

These amendments prohibited open-air testing, procurement of delivery vehicles, and back-door spending on chemical and biological warfare production. They required the Secretary of Defense to report to Congress on the program, the Surgeon General to make determinations that testing was not hazardous to the public, and called for consultation with both foreign nations and Congress on key issues such as the deployment and storage of the chemicals. Provisions to require safe procedures in shipping were also added to the bill.

By a unanimous vote, Senator Joseph D. Tydings, of Maryland, cut $25 million from the contingent funds for research. Senator J. William Fulbright, of Arkansas, reduced by $45 million the research funds spent by the military on social science and nonmilitary programs in the think tanks around the country and in overseas universities.

Three amendments I proposed passed unanimously. The first required annual disclosure of their former duties on weapons systems by high-ranking military and civilian employees of the Pentagon who went to work for defense contractors holding more than $10 million a year in prime contracts with the military. It also covered the duties of former employees of the contractors who subsequently went to work for the Pentagon.

A second amendment called for a selective but detailed study of defense-contractor profits by the General Accounting Office (GAO). Over the years, some persons had claimed that these profits were high. Others, including former Secretary McNamara, had said they were low. But no objective, independent study to determine the facts had ever been made. My amendment gave the GAO the power to do the job. The level of profits would be determined not only on sales but also on capital investment.

Finally, the Senate adopted my amendment to cut next year's spending for what is called independent research and development, or IR&D, by one-fifth of the amount authorized

Independent research and development has no direct relationship to contracts for defense research. In fiscal year 1969, the Defense Department allowed contractors to charge some $685 million in overhead costs, which included research by the contractor for strictly commercial items, unrelated to military research or production; funds for bidding and proposal work by the contractor on nondefense contracts; and write-offs by defense contractors for a category called "other technical effort." These efforts did not have to be related in any way whatsoever to the defense work of the contractor. Under existing practices, a defense contractor could carry on commercial research, bid on commercial contracts, and produce technical products for his commercial business, and yet charge from 80 to 100 per cent of the individual costs as overhead on his defense work.

I stumbled on this state of affairs during a conference with Comptroller General of the United States Elmer Staats and immediately drafted the amendment to ensure that defense research and development funds were tied to explicit Defense Department needs. There then descended on Washington a massive industrial lobby against any change. But the nature of the write-off was so shocking that both Senator Stennis and Senator Thomas J. McIntyre, of New Hampshire, felt it important to take some action. I proposed that a ceiling of $468 million be placed on the funds allowed for next year. As $685 million had been spent the year before and the figure would no doubt have risen to $750 million except for the limitation, the amendment provided a savings—in the range of $217 to $282 million—over what might otherwise have been spent. The *New York Times* called the 85-to-0 vote by which the amendment passed "the biggest budgetary achievement of the critics." In the compromise between the House and Senate versions of the bill, the amendment was retained, but the ceiling was set at $545 million. I introduced a bill to reform IR&D procedures, on which Senators Stennis and McIntyre promised to hold hearings. This area stands in urgent need of reform. The General Accounting Office has vast quantities of materials it has collected on dubious IR&D spending practices. The favored contractors will fight in a determined fashion, but the introduction of a bill and the facts that flow from public hearings can lead to action.

No progress was made in the Senate on reducing spending on dubious weapons systems themselves. But, for the first time, even though they were less successful than efforts on procedural items, challenges were made to hardware items. Senator Thomas F. Eagleton, of Missouri, and Senator Hatfield delayed approval of funds for the main battle tank (MBT-70) until a study of its effectiveness could be made. This passed. The justification for the fifteenth carrier was vigorously but unsuccessfully challenged by Senators Walter Mondale, of Minnesota, and Clifford Case, of New Jersey. They did succeed in deleting the long-lead–time funds for a third new *Nimitz*-class carrier. My amendment, aimed at cutting off funds for Run B of the C-5A, was offered and debated, but decisively defeated. Senators George McGovern, of South Dakota, and Charles Goodell, of New York, challenged money for the manned bombers (AMSA). They, too, lost. But each of these unsuccessful challenges laid the groundwork for victories we are, I firmly believe, going to win in the future.

And this was only the beginning. The fight was carried to the military appropriation bill itself, which included the remainder of the $80 billion originally requested. The courage to criticize was infectious. Other members of Congress joined the ranks. The public was aroused. Opinion crystallized against the huge excesses as the enormity of the waste was understood.

But one season of debates won and lost and of new questions asked is not enough. Many other steps must be taken.

One of the things Congress needs most is more information made available in a more orderly style to balance the disproportionate emphasis on military answers to the diplomatic problems that it now receives.

At the present time, the Armed Services committees, meeting behind closed doors, receive the annual "posture statement" from the Secretary of Defense. It is the Secretary of Defense who delivers, and the Armed Services committees who receive on behalf of Congress, the outline of our strategic capabilities, estimates of those of any potential enemy, disclosures of our military strength, and the intelligence estimates of the threat posed by our adversaries. The Armed Services committees also receive the views of the Secretary of Defense on what reactions and weapons are needed to meet the threat of the "higher-than-expected" and the "greater-than-expected" threats from those quarters.

The annual posture statement deals almost exclusively with the military threat and the military response to such threats. The absence of an equally strong, forthright, and thorough "posture" statement delivered to the Foreign Relations Committee from the diplomatic arm of government has had the effect of placing undue emphasis on military answers to world events. This is a mistake.

Military men are honorable. They are brave and courageous. But they suffer from "tunnel vision" and see things almost exclusively from a military point of view. They are concerned about how to defend the nation *militarily* against a *military* attack. This is not surprising. Indeed, it is as it should be. The military response is their job, and they do it well. It is no attack on them to point out where the boundaries of their competence lie.

But the military point of view should not be the exclusive determinant of this nation's foreign policy. Knowingly or unknowingly, as former President Eisenhower said, that has been the effect of the massive power in the hands of the Pentagon. The world is far too complicated to allow such a one-dimensional approach to dominate U.S. policy.

That the annual posture statement is delivered by the Secretary of Defense to the Armed Services Committee epitomizes the excessive power exercised by the military establishment. This must be changed.

In the "Hearings on Economic Priorities and the Military Budget," conducted by the Subcommittee on Economy in Government, former Budget Director Charles Schultze proposed that an annual posture statement should be presented to the Congress and the country by the Secretary of State. He, not the Pentagon, should tell Congress what our basic foreign policy is. He should discuss and review before the Foreign Relations and Foreign Affairs committees such fundamental strategic assumptions as the "two-and-one-half-war" program. The Secretary of State should review before Congress our diplomatic and military commitments. He and the Foreign Policy committees should examine the myriad overseas military bases. He should assess the relative military and diplomatic strengths of ourselves and our adversaries. He should stress the areas of accommodation and negotiation as well as the areas of danger and threat from a potential adversary, which are now dwelt on almost exclusively by the military.

Foreign policy is now too much in the hands of the military. It should be returned to civilian control.

I firmly agree with Schultze that the foreign policy "posture statement" should predominate. The place of the military posture statement should be diminished—not discontinued, because it contains too much factual evidence and policy analysis to be discarded. It is and should continue to be highly useful in determining policy. But it should not monopolize the field or dominate discussion.

In addition, we should end such practices as that of Defense Department officials publicly opposing a moratorium on U.S. testing of multiple warhead missiles (MIRV's) on the ground that it "would diminish the prospects of a successful outcome" of arms limitation talks with Russia. Let Defense Department spokesmen comment on the technical problems of the MIRV before the Armed Services Committee. Let them give an assessment of the Soviet Union's missile strength. But let the President or the Secretary of State assess the effects of testing, moratoriums, or deployment of weapons on the potential success or failure of arms talks.

One further proposal, which Schultze and others have made, appears, superficially at least, to have a great deal to recommend it. This is that a new committee of Congress be created to review and analyze the issues concerned with broad national priorities.

Schultze proposed that "an appropriate institution should be created within the Congress to review and analyze the two posture statements (Defense and State) in the context of broad national priorities, and an annual report on the two statements should be issued by the Congress."

Schultze's use of the term "an appropriate institution" showed his awareness of the congressional politics involved in the establishment of a new committee. Although he did not specify its title more exactly, he did propose certain characteristics and functions for the new institution. He said:

> It should review the basic factors on which the military budget is based, in the context of a long-term projection of budgetary resources and national priorities.

It should have as one part of its membership, Senators and Congressmen chiefly concerned with domestic affairs, to assert the claims of domestic needs.

It should not concern itself primarily with the technical details of weapons systems, procurement practices and the like: while these are very important, they are the province of other Committees. It is the "national priorities" of the military budget which should be the essence of the new institution's charter.

Above all, it should have a top-flight, highly qualified staff. The matters involved do require final solution by the judgment of political leaders, but in the complex areas with which the new institution would deal, its deliberations must be supported by outstanding, full-time, professional staff work.

I concur in the purpose of this proposal and in most of the functions the institution should perform. However, Schultze himself made it clear that he did not know what form the "appropriate institution" should take. I have strong doubts about whether it is possible to establish a new committee whose members would harbor the critical views essential to its proper function.

The power of appointment to committees in both houses of Congress and by both parties in Congress is, to a dominant degree, lodged in the hands of those who support the military and hold relatively uncritical views of its operations. I greatly fear that a new committee would be dominated, with some notable exceptions, by the very members of existing committees who have seldom exercised their critical faculties over military spending. It would be packed by the congressional Establishment. Existing committees now exercising some critical function would be urged to cease and desist on grounds that the new body would perform the function.

Thus, while I sympathize with the proposal, my experience with the power of the congressional Establishment leads me to question whether it could work. I would want to see more details about the committee's composition and membership before advocating it.

What I think might be more useful is a proposal along the following lines. First, in January each year, there should be two posture statements presented to Congress. One should cover the diplomatic and foreign policy posture of the United States. The other should be on our military strategic posture. These statements should be delivered to the Foreign Relations and Armed Services committees in the House and Senate, respectively.

Second, the President's annual Economic Report should contain a thorough and detailed analysis and recommendations on the priorities of the country both *between* civilian and military needs and the relative priorities *within* the civilian and military sectors. It should also give a thorough analysis of the effects of military spending. This "Priorities Posture Statement" could be presented to the Joint Economic Committee, which already has jurisdiction over the general subjects involved.

Third, each committee should hold short hearings in which distinguished proponents and critics of the posture statements would be heard. Each committee should then report to the House or Senate during the month of March. At that point, the leadership of the House and Senate should set a time, preferably under a unanimous consent agreement, providing for one or two days of debate on foreign and military policy issues and their relation to national priorities.

The chairman and ranking member of each committee should make a formal presentation of thirty minutes or less. Members of the key committees and other members of the House and Senate should be given time to express their views. Rebuttal by the principals should follow at the end of the debate.

In this way, national attention could be focused on the

vital issues. The expression of majority and minority views should be encouraged. With key posture statements and hearings to develop the issues and a two-day debate to resolve them, some sense of a national consensus would no doubt emerge from the airing of these most vital public issues.

Fourth, the Joint Economic Committee should develop the kind of top-flight, highly qualified staff that Schultze proposed. Not only its findings on weapons-systems procurement and the relative efficiency of spending funds on one weapon as against another, but also its analysis of economic, social, and budgetary priorities should be presented to Congress, especially to the Armed Services and Foreign Relations committees. This could be done during their detailed hearings on the substance of the President's budget and economic requests.

Presently, most hearings on the budget are exclusively one-sided. Only the advocates appear. Except to the degree that very busy members of the House and Senate can spend hours in the detailed review of an agency's budget, there is little cut and thrust. Generally, a handful of congressmen and one or two staff men are pitted against an entire agency. They do remarkably well. Congress should make no attempt to duplicate in numbers the size of the bureaucracy.

But if a top-flight congressional analytical staff could provide committees with the results of its work and if, then, the General Accounting Office could be called upon to tell Congress where the bodies are buried, analyze detailed requests critically, and create an adversary hearing, the Congress and the country would be greatly benefited.

Finally, the Senate Armed Services Committee should continue the practice it initiated in 1969 when Senator Stennis established a series of subcommittees to break down the initial $23 billion military authorization request into manageable portions. They responded to those critical views which individual members of Congress and the Joint Economic Committee had developed earlier, and a $3 billion cut by the Senate was the result.

These five points would, I think, carry out the spirit of Schultze's proposal, but would do it in the framework of existing congressional institutions. As a practical matter, that is the only way of getting it done.

There is one more reform needed, however, before Congress can mend its ways. Obvious as it is, it bears stating.

Fundamentally, Congress reflects to an inordinate degree the attitudes of the country. The pressures from local communities, Chambers of Commerce, trade unions, universities, and political figures are the main reason congressmen and senators act as they do. The ability of the public to urge budget cuts in general but oppose any budget cuts affecting their area or the institutions with which they are connected is one of the wonders of the world.

Members of Congress can only exercise their critical faculties if the public will back them up. Real change in public opinion is the only way to bring to an end the tradition of Congress as a pushover for the Pentagon.

VI

Men in the
Military-Industrial Complex
Part One: Civilians in the Pentagon

ON DECEMBER 30, 1960, former Senator Paul Douglas of Illinois, my predecessor as chairman of the Joint Economic Committee and the chairman of the Economy in Government Subcommittee (then the Subcommittee on Defense Procurement), addressed a letter to Secretary-designate of the Department of Defense, the Honorable Robert S. McNamara.

Douglas and other members of the Joint Economic Committee, including myself, were shocked at Pentagon extravagance. But successive secretaries of Defense had ignored the Committee's pleas. The Pentagon was disdainful and arrogant.

Douglas and the Committee prepared a bill of particulars based on our hearings and staff work.

Item: 86 per cent of all contracts—both in dollars and num-
         bers—were negotiated rather than let by competitive
         bidding.

Item: Over fifty General Accounting Office reports in the
         previous two years alone had pinpointed bad practices
         and malpractices in specific contracts for supplies. The
         waste added up to hundreds of millions.

Item: There was vast overlapping and duplication among the
         supply systems themselves. Each service had its own
         system with its individual personnel, inventories, and
         warehouses.

Item: There were huge accumulations of excess stocks in the
         service stock funds. Each service operated them in
         different ways. At times their upkeep involved a double
         appropriation—one to buy the items for the fund, an-
         other for the using service to get them out.

Item: The amount and disposal of surplus property was scan-
         dalous. Some $8 to $10 billion a year was sold off at 2
         to 3 cents on the dollar.

Item: There was vast concurrent buying and selling of sup-
         plies—one agency of the government in the market for
         new supplies while another agency was disposing of the
         same item as surplus. A Douglas-sponsored study
         showed this situation occurred in two-thirds of the
         cases for common supplies, even when the same item
         was available in the same geographic area.

The letter to Secretary-designate McNamara called the
condition in the system of procurement and supply "appalling" and "scandalous."

Unlike his predecessors, who had greeted such charges by
ignoring or denying them, McNamara acted. In March, he
met in his Pentagon office with the Comptroller-General, the
Director of the Budget Bureau, key members of the Joint
Economic Committee, and other members of Congress, including speaker John McCormack and Congressman F. Ed-

ward Hébert—who, in the past, had shown great interest in reforming the system of procurement and supply.

With the delegation seated around the huge table in his Pentagon office overlooking the Potomac, McNamara took up the points in order. After only two months on the job in the suite above the Mall Entrance to the Department of Defense, he gave a brilliant exposition of the problems. He understood them. He impressed the delegation with his perception and knowledge. It was obvious that he had done his homework.

Not only did he explain the problems. He proposed a specific course of action for solving each of them. That room, with its portrait of James V. Forrestal peering down on the group, had never seen anything quite like Secretary McNamara's performance.

He said that he would increase the amount of competitive bid contracts and reduce the number of cost-plus, fixed-fee awards. He set goals and spelled out the timetables to meet them. He would reduce the time allowed for action on General Accounting Office reports from six months to ninety days. He was prepared to have an outside group—Congress, the GAO, or the Budget Bureau—make an independent judgment that the actions he ordered were, in fact, carried out by the military services. He would reduce the amount of surplus property generated and raise the amounts received for the surplus sold off. He would make an intensive study of the overlapping supply systems.

Later, under the Committee's urging and with its warm public support, he integrated the three service supply systems into a common Defense Supply Agency. He took similar actions in forming the Defense Intelligence Agency and the Defense Communications Agency.

He asked the congressional group to meet with him on a regular basis both to suggest means of improving procurement and supply and to judge what had been done. Senator

Douglas, Speaker McCormack, the Comptroller-General, and others were deeply impressed. Finally, it seemed, the Pentagon had a man who could get the job done.

And act, McNamara did. He reduced the percentage of cost-plus, fixed-fee contracts from a peak of 38 per cent in 1961 to 9.4 per cent by the end of 1965. Formally advertised contracts increased from 12.2 per cent in fiscal year 1962 to a high of 17.6 in fiscal year 1965. Savings of 25 cents on the dollar were claimed. Contracts awarded on the basis of price competition went up from 33 per cent to 44.5 per cent from fiscal year 1961 to 1966. McNamara claimed savings of 10 cents on the dollar for shifts from no-price competition to some form of price competition.

A five-year cost-reduction program was instituted. Over that period, McNamara claimed savings of $14 billion. To skeptics, he proposed that the General Accounting Office, an independent agency, review and audit the program.

During his six and one-half years, he closed or consolidated some 967 military activities, released 1.8 million acres of real estate, sold 66 industrial plants, eliminated 207,000 job positions, and claimed $1.5 billion a year savings from these actions alone. Secretary McNamara also claimed that during the period no employee was separated without an offer of another job.

Along the way, he occasionally stubbed his toe. He pushed the highly controversial TFX contract, which went to General Dynamics, whose home base was in Texas. Then he hotly defended it before Senator John L. McClellan's Government Operations Committee's Subcommittee on Investigations. His defenders argue that he was told to do so, despite the fact that four military source selection boards had said it should go to Boeing.

Although he stopped production of the XB-70 bomber, postponed development of the AMSA over fierce Air Force opposition, stalled the Sentinel ABM, and canceled the mis-

sile-firing turrets on the M-60 tank, huge overruns nevertheless occurred under his administration. The rise in costs of
Minuteman II by $4 billion, the $2 billion C-5A overrun,
the rise in the cost of the carrier *Nimitz* from $150 to $600
million—all happened under McNamara's stewardship. The
conclusions of the Stubbing report that acquisition of major
weapon systems, when measured by the rise in their cost,
lateness in delivery, and failure to function efficiently, were
worse in the 1960's than during the 1950's is a heavy criticism of Secretary McNamara.

But opinions about him differ widely. Many believe he
was the best Secretary of Defense we have ever had. Before
1965, when the Vietnam War began to consume almost all of
his energies, he had vastly improved the Defense Department.
The very useful annual posture statement, with its detailed
analysis of our strategic position, was a peculiar McNamara
innovation. Under him, budgets had leveled off at about $50
billion per year. Yet the military fighting posture was far
more efficient than before. In combat-ready divisions, airlift
capacity, fighter squadrons, navy ship construction, the increase in numbers of both strategic and tactical nuclear warheads, the submarine program, and in almost every other
way, defense forces were bigger, better, stronger, and readier
than they had been when he entered office.

His critics form two schools. The traditional leaders of the
military services and their ultraconservative allies roundly
condemn McNamara and almost all that he stood for. They
are scathing in their denunciation of the former Secretary.
His name is anathema to them as Franklin D. Roosevelt's was
to a Wall Street board room.

On the other hand, critics of excessive Pentagon power
claim he created an efficient monster that is now out of
control.

"When Secretary McNamara took office," former Kennedy
White House aide Richard Goodwin has said, "it was with

the avowed aim of establishing greater civilian control over the military. Yet, the harsh fact of the matter is that when he left, the military had greater influence over American policy than at any time in our peacetime history."

At a Congressional Conference on the Military Budget and National Priorities, Goodwin elaborated his strong charges: "In the war game rules and around the conference table," he said, "we developed our options in the name of flexibility— amphibious forces, airborne forces, helicopter forces, special forces—seemingly unaware that when you have the ability to do something you will become powerfully tempted to do it."

Goodwin claimed the blame did not lie with the generals. "Force is their business," he said. "It was rather the civilian leadership which created this machine and gave it the tools to justify and explain and provide both the logic of fear and that exotic language of strategic theory which is used to baffle common sense."

That is the indictment from the Left. History will have to record the Secretary's record with respect to Vietnam and our military posture. But there is one clear failure, the major failure of the 1960's, which McNamara must share with the President, the Budget Bureau, Congress, and the General Accounting Office: The process of acquiring weapons systems was never brought under critical control. Because of this failure, we lost control of the military budget.

What weapons do we really need? What should we pay for them? How long should it take to deliver them? How effectively will they function? These questions were never answered properly.

Secretary McNamara did make a greater effort to answer them than anyone else had done. He instituted the Office of Systems Analysis in the Office of the Secretary of Defense, the famous "Whiz Kids" or "McNamara's Band."

Occasionally, the Whiz Kids got caught up in their own arrogance. It was amazing with what alacrity they were able to accept the press and intellectual community's superlatives about themselves. But the fact that their office existed prevented matters from getting worse than they did. An occassional weapons system was stopped. Others were postponed. Essentially, however, the military got its way.

In one particular stage, the review process broke down completely. Secretary McNamara and his procurement experts, specifically DOD Comptroller Charles J. Hitch and DOD Assistant Secretary for Installations and Logistics Thomas D. Morris, placed far too much emphasis on the self-controlling aspects of the contract-incentive system they devised. It was their contention that Defense Department supervision could end when a weapon-system contract was signed—a form of "disengagement" over weapons-system costs. They said the nature of the incentive contracts would prevent runaway costs, late delivery, and diluted specifications.

The system did not work. Neither incentive contracts nor "total package procurement" nor other gimmicks such as value engineering or PERT (Program Evaluation Review Technique!) or PEP (Program Evaluation Performance!) did the job. There was no substitute for the detailed day-to-day fiscal controls that the Defense Department managers abandoned. Almost total dependence was placed on the form of the contract. The daily "ditch-digging" was foregone. This colossal failure reached its zenith under Assistant Secretary of the Air Force Robert H. Charles and the C-5A procurement.

But, given the size of the job, the power of the economic forces, and the dangers in the world, Secretary McNamara came closer to mastering the job than any of his predecessors.

Robert S. Benson's article in the *Washington Monthly,* to which I have referred earlier, raised some obvious questions about McNamara's stewardship. Benson, formerly one of McNamara's Band, detailed some $9 billion in specific budget cuts he believed could be made without impairing our security or affecting U.S. forces in Vietnam. He, therefore, proposed that the cuts be made in those forces or systems that duplicated others, where any enemy threat was no longer credible, or where money was being lost through grossly inefficient performance.

"If all these Pentagon budget cuts are so obvious," he asked, "why didn't the cost-conscious McNamara regime push them through? Did the Whiz Kids fail? Were they really trying?" And he answered, "I think a fair assessment would have to conclude that they were trying hard, but were only partly successful." In retrospect, it appears that the Whiz Kids were too cocky and vastly underestimated their foes. Benson wrote that McNamara's Band "was greatly outnumbered by experienced adversaries bound together by a shared goal— more and bigger military programs." He claimed that the combination of pressures from the military, wanting expanded power, from industry, wanting greater sales and profits, and from Congress itself, responding to pressures from contractors and military employees, "made life difficult even for a man as strong and courageous as Robert McNamara."

Second, he said, the "Whiz Kids chose to concentrate on the relatively uncluttered strategic programs instead of digging into the fat and messy activities." He charged also that they "overdefended" positions once arrived at and cited an example, which became vital in the fight over the C-5A, that gives an interesting insight into the way weapons systems are approved.

"The current structuring of our programmed airlift/sealift needs," Benson wrote, "emanates from a carefully developed linear programming model." This model, he went on to explain, attached a high value to rapid deployment. It stemmed from an early 1960's Europe-oriented study showing high benefits in terms of "political bargaining power and casualty minimization." The analysis, he said, "still makes good sense in Europe, but now appears grossly misapplied in Asia. Yet nothing has been done to revise the high value placed on rapid deployment." (Almost a decade later, the consequences of this outmoded study were felt in the debate over the authorization of funds for the C-5A. It was the main strategic basis on which the need for the plane was based.)

Benson also cited the ability of the military proponents of approved weapon systems to escalate requirements, saying that carrying out the purchase of submarines or fighter planes "is not like walking into an automobile showroom and asking for a yellow Plymouth Belvedere sedan with power steering. As a submarine is built, many unanticipated choices present themselves; they involve different levels of effectiveness or convenience for different levels of dollars."

In any balance, one must concede that Secretary McNamara revolutionized the Pentagon. He was highly successful in improving the supply and logistics system. But he was largely unsuccessful in controlling contracts and funds for weapons systems and procurement. He greatly added to the military strength and efficiency of the United States. Until the Vietnam War, he did this at much smaller cost than it otherwise might have been done. But, from 1965 on, he made major misjudgments about the costs of the Vietnam War. Some say he was wrong on his estimates of military success. For this, however, the basic responsibility seems to lie with others, including the generals in the field whose optimistic assumptions never proved true. Giving full weight to both his strength and weaknesses, it seems clear that the eighth Secretary of Defense was the most competent and efficient of the men who, until his time, had presided at the Pentagon. Often, he displayed an extra dimension of perception. His descriptions of the nuclear arms race and its apocalyptic consequences were compelling. He believed, himself, that his "principal accomplishment was to educate the people that a strategic war cannot be won."

McNamara's successor, Melvin R. Laird, is a less complex,

equally competent man. A highly representative Midwestern Republican congressman, he was elected to the Wisconsin State Senate at 25, after distinguished service in the Navy during World War II, to fill the unexpired term of his father, a retired Presbyterian minister. He was sent to Congress from Wisconsin's Seventh District in 1952 and served principally on the House Appropriations Committee and its Defense Subcommittee. There, he distinguished himself as a man of great diligence and intelligence. He was one of the few members with the strength of mind and character to tangle on even terms with Secretary McNamara. Because of his strong views on defense matters, his appointment as Secretary of Defense was welcomed by the military services. This was in marked contrast to their lukewarm, sometimes hostile attitude toward Robert S. McNamara. Yet Laird is a man who is not overawed by the military establishment. He will not be bullied or browbeaten by either the services, claiming superiority of military knowledge, or Congress. He knows and understands both very well.

In McNamara and Laird, the country has had the services of two unusually competent men who can not be stereotyped or cast in a preconceived mold—steadfast men who run their own show and have the ability to claim respect even from their adversaries.

When the Department of Defense was organized and the three military services unified, the then Secretary of the Navy vigorously opposed the merger. James V. Forrestal, the man President Truman selected as the first Secretary of Defense, told the Senate Military Affairs Committee he did not believe that "the head of the proposed governmental colossus to be called the Department of National Defense will ever have more than the most superficial knowledge of the Department." He concluded that "He would be entirely in the hands of his military advisers."

Later, he said, "The plan . . . amounts to an isolation and derogation of the civil authority."

In the late 1960's, this view of a tough-minded Wall Street lawyer was echoed by Richard Goodwin, a speechwriter for President Kennedy, when he said, "In the name of efficiency we unified the operations of the armed services, introduced the techniques of computer management and encouraged closer interactions between the military and industry." Goodwin concluded, "As a result, power once checked by rivalries and inefficiency is now wielded as a single force defying effective democratic control."

Ten men have served as Secretary of Defense. Two of them, Clark Clifford and Thomas S. Gates, Jr., served too short a time for their stewardship to be judged. But Clifford, in his reversal of Vietnam policy, and Gates, in his grip on procurement and supply, laid the groundwork for significant change. At this writing, Secretary Laird has occupied the role for too short a time for his career to be judged. Although a hard-liner, he gives no indication of being taken over by the military, wearing any service's collar, or lacking knowledge of Pentagon activities.

Of the seven secretaries of Defense who had time to make their mark, four—Forrestal, General George C. Marshall, Robert A. Lovett, and McNamara—were decidedly superior men. Of the remaining three, Louis Johnson left after an untimely proposal to slash an already small military budget just before the North Koreans launched their invasion of South Korea. Charles E. Wilson and Neil H. McElroy, whose careers at the Pentagon were undistinguished, served under Eisenhower—a President who was, himself, never overawed by the military because of his own close relationship with the services. None of the civilian bosses of the Pentagon ever approached being "in the hands of his military advisers." Although military spending is now out of control, no devil theory could reasonably be applied to anyone who has served as Secretary of Defense. None was in any way an evil or malevolent force.

Short of the Presidency itself, the job of Secretary of Defense is the biggest job in the country. Because of the importance of the position, secretaries of Defense are selected with special care and for dimensions of character and personality beyond those of ordinary men. More often than not they grow in office. They are men whose ambitions are fulfilled, who are honored by the appointment, and who are sustained in the job by the awesome responsibility to protect the security of the United States.

This is not necessarily the case with the men who fill lesser positions at the Pentagon. There, different patterns emerge, and the situation is not so reassuring. There, the more parochial dangers ascribed to the military-industrial complex have an opportunity to flourish.

The typical career of an assistant secretary of one of the three services runs roughly like this. After graduation from a major Eastern university or an Ivy League law school, he joins either a Wall Street financial firm or a major New York or Washington law office. After an apprenticeship in New York, he moves to one of the major military contractors in the office of the general counsel or handles their business in Washington from the complex of firms located within walking distance of the White House. In his late thirties or early forties, he joins the Pentagon as an assistant secretary. The names change when the White House changes political complexion, but the men, their training, their background, their outlook, and their general demeanor do not.

In recent years, two additional groups have been woven into the Pentagon pattern.

One is the new breed of captive scientists and science-administrators who alternatively serve the Pentagon, the weapon-system contractors, or the university outposts of the military-industrial complex.

The situation that formerly existed at MIT best illustrates the interconnection between the universities and the Pentagon. Its two key defense institutions, the Instrumentation Laboratory and the Lincoln Laboratory, were involved in critical research on strategic weapons. Research on the MIRV system for use on the Poseidon missile was one of the Instrumentation (or "I") Lab's thorny problems; Lincoln Lab was just as deeply involved in anti-ballistic-missile (ABM) research. MIT has many interlocking directorates with the big contractors, as well. Of the top seventy-five Pentagon contractors, nineteen are represented on the MIT Corporation, including a director of Lockheed, the prime contractor for the Poseidon missile. No less than seven members of MIT's Corporation are directors, board chairmen, or presidents of AT&T or its key units, one of which, Western Electric, is the prime contractor for the Safeguard ABM system.

To head its military research, MIT hired Jack Ruina directly from the Pentagon complex. His successive jobs before joining MIT were Deputy for Research to the Assistant Secretary of the Air Force, Assistant Director for Defense Research and Engineering in the Office of the Undersecretary of Defense, Director of the Defense Department's Advanced Research Project Agency, and finally, President of the heavily Pentagon-supported think tank, the Institute for Defense Analyses (IDA). His MIT title is Vice President for Special Laboratories.

The second group—and one predominant in the pattern—is made up of Pentagon time-servers, the bureaucratic elite. These are the supergrade civil servants who occupy the key positions from era to era. They are the men for all seasons, the faceless men who, long ago, made peace with their consciences and whose adaptability is their main virtue. They are not the secretaries, under secretaries, and assistant secretaries, although very occasionally, after long tenure and service distinguished primarily by their ability to survive, they are promoted to one of the major positions. They are the enduring third and fourth echelon. Secretaries of Defense may come and secretaries of Defense may go, but the deputy assistant to the assistant secretary stays on forever.

There is yet another group that holds extraordinary power. The recruitment of men to fill key civilian posts at the Pentagon from the ranks of the officers, employees, or representatives of the nation's biggest defense contractors has unfortunately been a common and expected practice. The examples are legion.

David Packard is the present Deputy Secretary of Defense. This is the second highest job in the Department. Packard owns 3.5 million shares of the 12.5 million shares of the Hewlett-Packard Company, which does millions of dollars of business annually with the Defense Department. Before his appointment, he served as a director of the General Dynamics Corporation, when it was the number one defense contractor in the country, with about $2.3 billion in prime military contracts. He was also a director of the United States Steel corporation, which is now 56th on the list of the 100 largest defense contractors. In addition, he served as a director of the Stanford Research Institute, which performs almost $30 million a year in Defense Department contracts for research, development, tests, and evaluation. Packard did not dispose of the $300 million he owned in Hewlett-Packard stock when he took office but, with the consent of the Senate Armed Services Committee, established a charitable trust.

The issues surrounding his nomination were well put by Hobart Rowen, the *Washington Post* economics and finance writer. Rowen called it a "conflict of attitude." After alluding to the stock-ownership question, Rowen wrote:

My argument was—and is—that in addition to a conflict of interest because he proposed to keep (in trust) his $300 million of Hewlett-Packard stock, his appointment raises again, in a very specific way, the question of the military-industrial "complex" and its powerful role in shaping policy as the world turns increasingly to nuclear weapons.

That part of the U.S. industrial machine closely tied to defense spending has an enormous stake in seeing a continuance of big military budgets . . . so the question must be raised as to Packard's ability to view impartially not only questions that may relate to his own company, but to the whole philosophy of defense spending.

Professor Edward N. Beiser, of the Political Science Department at Brown University, put it well, too, in a letter to the editor of the *New York Times:*

The problem . . . is that whatever financial arrangements he makes, Mr. Packard cannot and will not divest himself of his many friends, contacts and enemies in defense industries, and of the values and attitudes he has developed as a defense producer. The crucial conflict of interest results from the overlapping directorate being developed by the defense establishment inside and outside of Government.

I intend no personal charge against Secretary Packard. His case merely illustrates the point. This was precisely the objection I raised on the floor of the Senate to the 2,100 former high-ranking military officers who left the Pentagon to work for the hundred largest defense contractors. The point is the same whether a military or a civilian is involved. It is the same whether an officer leaves the Pentagon to work for the contractors or a contractor leaves his business to take an important post at the Pentagon.

A similar situation existed with Roswell L. Gilpatric, who served as Deputy Secretary of Defense from 1961 to 1964. A member of the law firm of Cravath, Swaine, and Moore, when he became deputy to McNamara in 1961, he and his firm had represented General Dynamics in the period 1958–61. Gilpatric's fees had exceeded $100,000. Although he left his firm, he continued to receive some $20,000 a year in severance pay while at the Pentagon. In the meantime, Cravath, Swaine, and Moore continued to represent General Dynamics.

Like Packard, Deputy Secretary of Defense Gilpatric had been a part of the military–industrial–law firm complex for years. He had served as Under Secretary of the Air Force in 1951–53 and as chairman of the Board of Trustees of the nonprofit Aerospace Corporation that President Eisenhower established to conduct studies on major missile systems.

The storm and furor over Gilpatric's relationships were raised during the TFX investigation. It was shown that he had taken a direct part in the negotiations over the highly controversial contract, which went to General Dynamics. He was involved in discussions on the contract. He signed the letter turning down Senator McClellan's request that the formal signing with General Dynamics be delayed.

Fred Korth, Secretary of the Navy in 1962, is another case in point. He had a past close relationship with the Defense Department and with the defense contractors and played a questionable part in the TFX controversy as well.

His official Pentagon biography states that he rose from a second lieutenant to lieutenant-colonel in the Air Transport Command during World War II. After private law practice in Fort Worth, in 1951 he became Department Counselor, Department of the Army. In 1952, he was made an Assistant Secretary of the Army. He returned to Fort Worth where he was elected executive vice president and director of the Continental National Bank and, later, became its president. He was a director of the Bell Aerospace Corporation and active in the Navy League of the United States.

Korth succeeded John B. Connally, Jr., another Texan from Fort Worth, as Secretary of the Navy. When Korth was approved by the Senate Armed Services Committee, he stated that he had resigned as president of the Fort Worth Continental National Bank. But he retained his stock valued at $160,000 in the bank and told the Committee he intended to return to the bank when he left public office. Only a few months before he was appointed, Korth had approved a

$400,000 loan from his old bank to the General Dynamics Corporation. The Convair plant of General Dynamics was in Fort Worth. Although $400,000 may not appear to be a large sum for the largest defense contractor in the country to borrow, it was, nonetheless, two-thirds of the $600,000 loan limit allowed the small Continental National Bank.

As Secretary of the Navy, Korth made the decision about the TFX. The Pentagon's Source Selection Board had recommended that the contract go to Boeing. Korth overruled the Board and recommended General Dynamics. Along with Secretary McNamara and Air Force Secretary Eugene Zuckert, Navy Secretary Korth signed the five-page memorandum of justification.

The question of a conflict of interest was raised directly with the Justice Department by Senator John J. Williams, of Delaware. In fairness to both Korth and Gilpatric, the Justice Department wrote that in their opinion there was no law violation in either Korth's or Gilpatric's role in the TFX contract.

Later, Korth was so indiscreet as to write letters promoting the business of the Continental National Bank on Navy Department stationery. He resigned shortly after this matter was drawn to the attention of Attorney General Robert Kennedy by Senator McClellan.

The Korth case had overtones of the Harold Talbott case. Talbott, Secretary of the Air Force in the Eisenhower Administration, had written to defense contractors on his official Air Force stationery soliciting business for an industrial management firm in which he remained as a "special partner."

The conflicts of interest of former Secretary of the Navy Korth and Secretary of the Air Force Talbott are unique, and the ethical questions raised by Deputy Secretary of Defense Gilpatric's TFX role and Secretary Packard's retention of his $300 million in Hewlett-Packard stock are far from

everyday occurrences. Not so the intimate relationship between other high Pentagon civilians and the big contractors. The list of such relationships is almost limitless.

The facts do not imply illegal relationships. Often, they
do not even imply improper relationships. The fact that
Secretary McNamara was President of the Ford Motor Company, the fifth ranking military contractor when he took over
at the Pentagon, implies neither an illegal nor unethical
relationship. In his case, he disposed of all of his Ford stock at a
huge personal financial sacrifice.

But when former Assistant Secretary of Defense for Installations and Logistics Thomas D. Morris went directly
from the Pentagon to work for Litton Industries, I thought
that serious ethical questions were involved.

When Tom Morris was in charge of all Defense Department contracts and procurement, Litton Industries was the
fourteenth biggest defense contractor in the country. It did
$465.7 million dollars of business annually with the Penta-
gon. In fact, the contracts had grown from $180 million the
year before, or by 250 per cent. Litton was one of the giant
new conglomerates. At least twelve of its subsidiaries did
business with the military. The lion's share of Litton's business was done by the Ingalls Shipbuilding Corporation with
$277 million and Litton Systems, Inc., with $150 million of
annual defense contracts. The latest figures show Litton with
$317 million in defense business, of which Litton Systems
had the lion's share, with $292 million.

In fairness to Morris, it must be said that he was a hard-
working, tireless Assistant Secretary of Defense. He claims he
had no direct contact with Litton Industries while at the
Pentagon. Furthermore, he asserts that a part of the understanding he had with the company was that he was to take no
part in defense business. The division of Litton with which
he was to serve as vice president did only a token amount
of defense contracting. All of that is true.

Nevertheless, I believe it was an unfortunate action for him to take the job. Morris will have had powerful associations with virtually every Pentagon high procurement official who deals with Litton or approves their contracts. He will have hired or promoted Pentagon officials who will deal with Litton in the future. In these days of "negotiated" contracts, awards are widely determined by the subjective attitudes of those at the Pentagon. I think it was a mistake in judgment.

It is not as if there were no other place to work. A man as able as Morris can choose among jobs. There is an old saying that where the public's business is concerned one must not only do right, one must also appear to do right. That is why I thought Tom Morris made a mistake in what he did.

The Administration itself made an enormous mistake along similar lines when, on June 30, 1969, President Nixon and Secretary of Defense Laird jointly announced the formation of a special blue-ribbon panel to study the procurement and management practices of the Pentagon. This panel, which, they said, they hoped would "restore public confidence and credibility in the Department of Defense," was so heavily weighted with members of the industrial side of the military-industrial complex that it could scarcely be expected to have such a comforting effect.

But, in this case, the error was more serious than mere failure to give the appearance of doing right. A close examination of its members' connections with the Pentagon explains why.

Gilbert W. Fitzhugh, Chairman of the Board of Metropolitan Life Insurance Company, and a member of the Board of Directors of the Singer Company and Consolidated Edison, was selected to head up the panel. At the time of Fitzhugh's appointment, Metropolitan Life had outstanding loans to twenty-four top defense contractors valued at almost $1.4 billion and held over $34 million worth of common stock in companies among the top 100 defense contractors. Despite this fact, Secretary Laird confidently assured the nation that "under Mr. Fitzhugh's leadership the Panel will view the Department of Defense with a fresh, objective, and uninvolved perspective."

The *New York Times* commented on the announcement by saying: "Companies that do business with the Pentagon were heavily represented in the group." It seemed that the selection of Fitzhugh as Chairman had set the pattern for the selection of the other members.

Of the sixteen panel members selected, nine of the members, representing a majority of the panel membership, held official positions with thirteen different companies that had a combined total of over $1.8 billion in defense contracts or holdings. Moreover, a number of these members have held high-ranking military or civilian positions in the Defense Department before joining defense industries.

Heading the list of members with close Pentagon associations was Robert C. Jackson, chairman of the board of Ryan Aeronautical Company. At the time of Jackson's appointment to the panel, Ryan was the twenty-third largest defense contractor, with defense business totaling almost $300 million. Almost 70 per cent of Ryan Aeronautical's business was with the Pentagon. Not only has Jackson's company had very important contracts with the Pentagon, but Jackson himself is a member of several DOD-related organizations. He is a member of the Aerospace Manufacturer's Council, the public relations arm of the Aerospace Industries Association, which represents the entire industry before the government and the public. He is a member of the Defense Orientation Conference Association, a group of top-flight business and professional leaders who receive regular briefings on Pentagon activity. Jackson also holds memberships in the Air Force Association, the Navy League, and the Army Aviation Association—all of which are heavy supporters of Pentagon policies.

George Champion, an outstanding supporter of Pentagon activity, is a director of the Traveler's Insurance Company, which has loans and stock interests in defense industries totaling almost $200 million. At the time of his appointment, Champion was a director of the International Paper Company, which held $665,000 worth of defense contracts, and of American Smelting and Mining Company, which had $448,000 worth of defense business. In addition, he holds positions with the Chase Manhattan Bank, the Chase International Investment Corporation, the Standard Bank, and the Standard Finance and Development Corporation—all companies that rely upon defense holdings for a considerable part of their business.

Following Champion is Lewis Franklin Powell, Jr., whose Richmond, Virginia, law firm, Hunton, Williams, Gay, Powell and Bibson, at the time of his appointment, represented Newport News Shipbuilding and Drydock Company, the thirty-fourth largest defense contractor, with $181 million worth of defense contracts. Almost 60 per cent of the company's business was with the Pentagon. At the time of his appointment, Powell was also a director of the Chesapeake and Potomac Telephone Company, which held over $13 million in defense contracts. Formerly an Air Force intelligence officer, Powell is a retired colonel in the Air Force Reserves.

Ruben F. Mettler has very close professional and business ties with the Pentagon and the defense industry. He is presently Executive Vice-President and a director of TRW Inc., which holds more than $170 million in defense contracts and ranks thirty-eighth on the top 100 list. Mettler is also Industry Vice-Chairman of the Defense Industry Advisory Council, a group of representatives from top defense contractors that meets several times a year to discuss procurement problems with Deputy Secretary of Defense David Packard. Mettler left Hughes Aircraft, another giant defense contractor, in 1954, to become a special consultant to the Assistant Secretary of Defense. He then went to TRW in 1955. Between 1958 and 1969, TRW rose from 89th to 38th on the top 100 list of defense contractors. On an earlier separate list of contractors doing research and development for the government, TRW stood in 17th position in 1968.

Wilfred J. McNeil is presently a director and advisor of the Fairchild-Hiller Corporation, which has $148 million in defense contracts, the nation's 43d largest defense contractor. Almost half of Fairchild-Hiller's business is with the Pentagon. Before coming to Fairchild-Hiller, McNeil served as a Pentagon employee for sixteen years from 1941 to 1957. By the time he left the Pentagon in 1957, he had attained the position of Assistant Secretary of Defense and Comptroller. He is presently a member of the Navy League, a group of retired naval officers, and a member of the Army-Navy Club. In short, McNeil's entire life, both professional and social, revolves largely around Pentagon-related organizations.

William Blackie is Chairman of the Board of the Caterpillar Tractor Company, which held nearly $43 million in defense contracts at the time of his appointment; one-fourth of the company's business was with the Defense Department. He is also a director of the Shell Oil Company, which, at the time, held close to $33 million in defense contracts.

William P. Clements, Jr., was Chairman of the Board of Governors of Southern Methodist University, which held $735,000 in defense contracts, when he was appointed to panel membership. Clements is also a director of the Fidelity Union Life Insurance Company, which has loans and stock interests in defense industries totaling $7.6 million. In addition, he is chairman of SEDCO, Inc., which, at the time of his appointment, held another $93,000 in defense contracts. The defense holdings of the First National Bank of Dallas, of which Clements is a director, are not public.

At the bottom of the list, and rounding out the majority of

the panel, is John Maurice Fluke, president of John Fluke Manufacturing Company, which held $1,472,000 worth of defense contracts at the time of his appointment.

Each of these eight men, in addition to Fitzhugh, on the average, represents interests of over $100 million in either defense contracts or defense-industry holdings. Taken together, they have a combined total of more than $1 billion worth of interests in defense contracts and defense industries. Even this figure, however, is dwarfed by Chairman Fitzhugh's interests in the Metropolitan Life Insurance Company alone.

Can Fitzhugh and these eight panel members seriously be expected to view the Department of Defense with a "fresh, objective, and uninvolved perspective"? The members of this panel, who are charged by the President with restoring confidence and credibility in the Pentagon, will be asked to view critically companies, possibly including their own, and to recommend changes in procurement policies. Nine of them may be faced with recommending changes that may hurt their own interests.

The remaining seven panel members are not plagued by direct personal interests in defense business, but a number of them lack the knowledge of defense procurement practices needed to counterbalance the long experience in these matters that the nine-man majority brings to the panel. Four of the seven have had almost no experience to prepare them to challenge the interests of the nine defense contractors represented on the panel: Hobart Durbin Lewis, president of the *Reader's Digest,* and a close friend of President Nixon; Martha Elizabeth Peterson, a career personnel dean who presently serves as president of Barnard College; Claude (Buddy) Young, a former professional football halfback and public relations man for beer companies; Leona Pouncey Thurman, a gifted lawyer from Kansas. All are undoubtedly competent in their respective fields, but can a woman's dean, a football player, a lady lawyer, and a magazine president be expected to challenge successfully the views on military procurement practices of the nine panel members who have spent their lifetimes in the defense business?

The only panel members who are not plagued by conflicts of interest, and who may be capable of balancing some of the influence of the nine defense contractors, are Dr. Marvin L. Goldberger, a competent physicist with extensive experience in test and evaluation work, Dr. George Joseph Stigler, a well-known conservative economist who has wide-ranging experience in budgeting matters, and Joseph Lane Kirkland, who is presently Secretary-Treasurer of the AFL-CIO and who will bring to the panel valuable knowledge regarding management practices.

Unfortunately, the membership of the panel is not the only or even the chief roadblock to an objective review of the Pentagon. Contracting and staffing procedures set up by the panel have virtually ensured that the final report will give present policy a resounding vote of confidence, possibly with minor reservations. The panel's top staff man is not an outside critic, but a Pentagon official. He is J. Fred Buzhardt, a graduate of the United States Military Academy and former aide to Senator Strom Thurmond. He is presently a special assistant to Assistant Secretary of Defense Robert Froehlke. In Froehlke's own words, Buzhardt is "my man Friday."

Despite this close relationship to a high Pentagon official, Buzhardt is to serve as chief administrative officer for the very panel which is studying, among other things, the activities of his regular boss. Buzhardt, thus, by the very definition of his roles, has a conflicting set of loyalties. I am unwilling to speculate as to whom he owes his first allegiance. His paycheck, however, continues to come from the Pentagon.

What's more, the Pentagon is loaning additional staff to the panel, and these staff members are remaining on the Department of Defense payroll. Although the Pentagon staff on loan consists primarily of clerical and security support, it is indicative of the unusual degree of "cooperation" that the Pentagon has been willing to extend to the work of the panel.

Even more serious than staffing is the problem of what areas of the Pentagon will be studied. The panel has negotiated a broad research contract with the Stanford Research Institute calling for the Institute to recommend study areas and potential research institutions to carry out the studies. Stanford will do some of the research work itself, and also will negotiate the contracts for the panel with other institutions. This is particularly important, because the character of the institutions that do studies for the panel will affect the results.

For many years, the Stanford Research Institute has been very dependent on the government, particularly the Defense Department, for the vast bulk of its research work. According to an article published in the November, 1966, issue of *Fortune* magazine, "the proportion of Stanford Research Institute's revenues derived from government contracts (including subcontracts) rose from 50 per cent in 1955 to 75 per cent in 1960." At the time it was picked, Stanford Research Institute was engaged in projects for the government valued at over $27 million. One of its more highly publicized contracts was an almost $2.5 million grant to do research and development on proving the feasibility of the ABM system. Even the Institute's own staff members have become concerned that the organization "was becoming an appendage of the government."

But the Stanford Research Institute's connection to the Pentagon runs even deeper than sheer economic dependence. Deputy Secretary of Defense David Packard served as a member of the Institute's Executive Committee, the steering group for the organization, from 1958 to January, 1969, when he assumed his present position. Exactly what role Packard had, if any, in the decision to employ the Stanford Research Institute as the panel's chief advisory and contracting agency is unknown. What is known, however, is that a number of the board members of the Institute are outstanding supporters of the Pentagon; some are currently serving as directors of the American Ordnance Association, a group of arms manufacturers and military personnel that advises the Pentagon on the industrial and military preparedness of the United States. Other directors of the Institute have been supporters and have contributed to such right-wing groups as the Americans for Constitutional Action, the Christian Anti-Communist Crusade, and For America. These directors serve as advisors on research efforts, publication, and staff commitments, as well as the hiring and firing of staff members. In view of the Institute's advisory role in the work of the panel, the influence of these directors may be substantial.

The inescapable impression one gets from all of this is that the panel is caught in the embrace of the very individuals whom it is supposed to evaluate and constructively criticize. Any objective criticism that comes out of the panel's work will, in all likelihood, be window dressing designed to hide the areas of glaring inefficiency untouched by the study. The panel has become another creature of the Pentagon, a product of the in-house management tactics for which the Defense Department is famous and that have doomed so many previous studies.

We have seen all this happen before. The script has become all too familiar. If highly critical, the final report will have a difficult time ever reaching the public print. If friendly, it will be carefully noted and thoroughly publicized for a few weeks, only to be relegated to the shelf once its publicity value for the Pentagon has been exhausted. Minor recommendations for change will be quickly accepted as "very valuable" by Pentagon officials and then promptly forgotten after the initial flurry of activity. The panel is, at best, a sham, at worst, an indication of how powerful the Pentagon has actually become—so powerful that it is able to control those who would criticize it.

Stronger measures than new studies, even studies less suspect than this one, are needed.

I have made two proposals to improve the general situation in defense contracting. The first is the disclosure amendment referred to in Chapter V. It provides that both high-ranking civilians and military personnel who work for the big military contractors have to make an annual disclosure giving details of the jobs they held at the Pentagon the three years before they left, and any contracts that they negotiated or made key decisions about. They also are required to report the contracts their new employers have with the military.

This requirement applies to all retired majors and above who go to work for a firm doing over $10 million a year with the Pentagon. It applies to all civilians of Civil Service Grade 13 or above who leave the Pentagon to work for major contractors. It also applies, in reverse, to key officials in the Pentagon who come to work for the Department from a major defense contractor.

The amendment provides that the information must be on file and open to inspection at the Pentagon to the press and public. It also requires the Secretary of Defense to make an annual report to the Congress listing, by company, names of the former officials, along with a summary of the information. Nominal penalties for failure to comply were included in the legislation.

The theory of the disclosure amendment is that sunlight is a great disinfectant. If a man is unwilling to see information about his job publicized, he should not take the job; the test is whether he would want it to appear in a newspaper column. It conforms to the practice in the British House of Commons that men may speak on an issue in which they are personally or financially involved, but are in contempt of the House if they fail to declare their interest.

I have also proposed a conflict-of-interest statute, which would apply to all departments of the U.S. Government. This bill would bar federal contracting or procurement officers from taking jobs with contractors or other direct beneficiaries of the contract that they have participated personally in granting, awarding, or administering, for a period of two years after leaving the government.

It may surprise many to learn, as it surprised me, that such a requirement is not already in the law.

VII

Men in the Military-Industrial Complex Part Two: Officers in Industry

THERE IS NO MORE ECONOMIC PRESSURE on a retired high-ranking military officer to force him to take a job with a big defense contractor than there is on a former high-ranking civilian in the Pentagon. Admirals and generals retire at very close to full basic pay. Colonels and Navy captains make out all right, too. The perquisites of free medical care, commissary shopping, and a variety of tax and service privileges continue. A grateful country has made generous provision for their retirement.

Yet, one of the most dangerous and shocking aspects of the military-industrial complex is the ease with which military officers retire and move into big jobs in the defense industries. It matches the way in which high-ranking civilians in defense or defense-related industries move into the Pentagon —and out again into industry. There is, in fact, an active, ever-working, fast-moving, revolving door between the Pentagon and its big suppliers.

We all know this in a general way. From time to time, individual reports about a former general or admiral heading up a big defense industry appear in the newspapers. Ex-generals turn up as Washington lobbyists. They request appointments with senators and congressmen. Occasionally, in former years, a Drew Pearson column exposed their activities. But no detailed data has been provided about them on a regular basis. In fact, it has been a decade since any comprehensive information has been supplied on this subject.

To provide a basis of solid fact for judging their influence, I wrote to the Secretary of Defense last year and asked him for a list of retired military officers of the rank of Navy captain or Army, Air Force, and Marine Corps colonel and above who worked for the 100 largest military contractors. At the same time, I sought data from the Library of Congress concerning high civilian officials in the Department of Defense, some of which has been reviewed in the chapter preceding this. The Pentagon itself has had this information about retired officers, but, for years, has refused to release it. Under a Department of Defense directive (5500.7, Section XVI-D-2-a, to be precise) each regular retired officer of the armed services must file with his branch of service a "Statement of Employment" within thirty days after retirement and keep it up to date.

But the Pentagon has kept the lid on this information. Reporters, writers, and ordinary citizens have been unable to get it. The Department of Defense could not refuse a request for it from a U.S. senator. However, rather than meet the request by merely compiling the data from their own records and sending it to me, the Pentagon officials did it the hard way. They sent messages to each of the top 100 contractors relaying my request and asking them for their own lists. Through this device, DOD bureaucrats could avoid setting a precedent. They could then continue to deny future requests for their own data from all but determined members of the House or Senate.

These lists from the individual contractors, then, rather than the Pentagon's own information, made up the initial information that was forwarded to me. Stacked on top of one another, the individual replies measured almost two inches thick. What I made public was what the contractors themselves provided. Any mistakes or errors were theirs, or the result of an unclear Pentagon request, not mine. These were the facts at the time I released the information.

The final completed lists showed that, as of February, 1969, some 2,124 former high ranking officers were employed by the 100 biggest military contractors. In fiscal year 1968, prime military contracts all told totaled $38.8 billion. The 100 biggest companies shared a $26.2 billion portion of the contracts in that fiscal year. This was 67.4 per cent of the total.

Ten companies alone, with contracts worth $9.5 billion, employed over half the total number of ex-officers, or 1,065 of them. Nine of the major defense contractors involved in research and development for the anti-ballistic-missile system had 465 retired officers on their payrolls.

Lockheed Aircraft, contractor for the C-5A, the Cheyenne helicopter, and the Navy submarine rescue vessel, employed 210 former officers, the largest number of them all. Remember that Lockheed's overrun on the C-5A was $2 billion. Its production contract for the Cheyenne helicopter was canceled after repeated failure. And the cost of the submarine rescue vessel it was building for the Navy went up from $3 million per unit to over $77 million each. This was, of course, not alone the fault of the high-ranking retired officers who worked for Lockheed. But it is symptomatic that the company with one of the worst efficiency records, if not the worst record of all the big companies, employed the largest number of former officers. It also paid one of the highest dividends per share of any major aerospace industry.

Boeing, famous for the SST, employed 169 officers. General Dynamics of TFX fame—now the F-111—held contracts worth $2.2 billion and had 113 former Navy captains, full colonels, and above on its payroll. North American Rockwell, which builds key components of the Minuteman missile, employed 104. Others in the top ten included General Electric, with 89; Ling-Temco-Vought, Inc., with 69; Westinghouse Electric, with 59; TRW, Inc., with 56; and Hughes Aircraft Company, with 55.

These ten companies averaged more than 106 former high-ranking officers per firm, with naval captains and bird colonels almost a dime a dozen. The big recruits were the generals and admirals.

Lockheed Aircraft Company, and its missile and space divisions, had no less than 22 admirals and generals in its various plants. The highest-ranking ex-officers, Admiral J. H. Sides and Army Lieutenant General W. W. Dick, Jr., were both designated "Senior Military Advisor." Rear Admiral P. E. Summers managed Lockheed's "Deep Quest" program— the program in which the original cost of the submarine rescue vessel increased by twenty-five times.

Former Air Force Lieutenant General L. C. Craigie and Lieutenant General L. I. Davis held the titles respectively, of Director of Requirements and Executive Secretary of the Corporate Safety Board. Former Vice Admiral C. C. Smith showed up as a management specialist in Lockheed's space system's advanced programs section. A proliferation of former Air Force, Marine Corps, Navy, and Army officers managed Lockheed's research and development programs, were vice presidents and general managers of various divisions, and managed the field service departments for the

C-5A and the C-141 airplane programs. Name the position. Lockheed had an ex-general, admiral, colonel or captain in the slot.

Boeing Aircraft, the firm with the second largest number of ex-officers, carried 15 admirals or generals on its rolls. One of them, former Army Brigadier General Glen O. Goodhand, was among Boeing's many "Washington representatives." That's another name for lobbyists.

Among the more controversial Boeing programs are the contract for the SST and the proposal for the new manned bomber, AMSA. The SST, or supersonic transport, is a commercial plane being built almost exclusively with huge government subsidies. With its destructive sonic boom, the SST cannot now be used at high speeds over heavily populated areas. Even if it works, it will save the jet set only a few hours between New York and London or Athens. At the present time, it would take almost as long to get to and from the center of major cities to the remote airfields required for its use as it would take to span the Atlantic. And, according to its critics, in this age of sophisticated missiles, the AMSA will be obsolete before it is ever built. If the Pentagon builds the 240 bombers it has proposed, the ultimate cost to the country could run as much as $20 billion. Boeing has huge interests at stake in these two programs.

It is not surprising, therefore, that a retired Air Force colonel is listed as Boeing's manager of the AMSA System Analysis and Customer Requirements Division. And who is the customer the Customer Requirements Division caters to? This plane carries no passengers. No TV ads to attract its clientele are necessary. No "Take Me Along" jingles are needed to entice wives to accompany their husbands on business trips at excursion fares. The AMSA is an Air Force plane. Equally unsurprising is the fact that a former Navy captain is the liaison officer and project engineer for the SST.

At McDonnell Douglas Aircraft, key military contracts included Air Force and Navy fighter planes, the AWACS continental air defense system, the manned orbiting laboratory (MOL), and the Spartan missile and other components of the ABM complex. This business is the company's bread and butter.

According to the lists, a retired Navy captain, Richard F. Kane, is "Quality Manager" for both the F-4 fighter plane and the completion of the new F-15 contract. A retired Navy captain, R. L. Cormier, is listed as Assistant Manager for the company's Navy programs under McDonnell Douglas's Military Systems Division. The manned orbiting laboratory (MOL) project attracted a bevy of retired Air Force colonels. McDonnell Douglas filled the AWACS continental-air-defense-system project with retired officers from a variety of services. In addition, former Air Force Major General O. J. Ritland was a vice president in charge of launch operations of McDonnell Douglas' astronautics company; Brigadier General M. C. Smith of the Air Force was operations manager for the same branch; and the director of Astronautics Management Systems was former Navy Rear Admiral B. A. Miles. At the company's general offices in Santa Monica, California, former Air Force Brigadier General R. W. Fellows was an assistant to the vice president for employee relations. In Los Angeles, retired Rear Admiral J. A. Thomas was director of McDonnell Douglas's international programs for military systems marketing.

The list goes on and on.

General Dynamics is famous for the TFX fighter plane and the huge controversy that engulfed it. Charges and countercharges of improper influence in its award accompanied the contract. In fairness, let it be said, they were aimed mainly at civilian influences in the Pentagon. Kleig light hearings were held by the Senate where Secretary McNamara and Senator John L. McClellan were the star attractions. The plane, now called the F-111, has been beset with problems. These include huge cost overruns, a series of unexplained crashes, and malfunctioning electronic equipment. Each plane now costs an estimated $12.5 million as compared with an initial estimate of $3.4 million. If we include spare parts, the Pentagon will spend $7.2 billion for 550 F-111's or about $13.1 million apiece.

Meantime, General Dynamics was not inattentive in its program for the care and feeding of retired high-ranking military officers. Retired Air Force General J. W. Kelly was in charge of its international staff in the Washington, D.C., office. The Washington office manager was retired Air Force Lieutenant General H. T. Alness. At Fort Worth, two retired generals and seven colonels were intimately involved in the F-111 program. All in all, General Dynamics employed 13 former generals or admirals, along with 100 colonels and former Navy captains. As expected, the admirals showed up in the Electric Boat Division or at Quincy, Massachusetts, as manager of ship systems (Rear Admiral James Reynolds), on the DD 963 program (Rear Admiral H. Reiter), and as director of engineering (Rear Admiral C. Palmer).

North American Rockwell is a huge aerospace company. It handles almost $700 million a year in defense contracts and many hundreds of millions of dollars more in space projects. On its payrolls is retired Air Force Lieutenant General W. A. Davis, who is a group vice president in charge of aircraft. Altogether, North American Rockwell employs 60 former high-ranking Air Force officers, of whom there were seven generals and 53 colonels. One of the latter, Colonel W. T. Wilborn, was project manager for Department of Defense projects. Another, Colonel D. J. Yockey, was director of the Astrionics Division. Colonel Yockey, about whom much more will be said later, merely switched hats and went directly from a key spot in the Air Force's Minuteman missile electronic brain project, which Rockwell handled, to the employ of the company. He retired from the Air Force in August, 1966, and in September, he went to work for the company.

North American Rockwell also had 24 former high-ranking Navy officers in its employ, including three admirals and 21 Navy captains. The fact that North American Rockwell does a lot less business with the Army than with the Air Force was reflected in the small number of former high-ranking Army officers hired by the company. The names of no Army generals and only nine colonels graced the payroll, as contrasted with the seven former generals and 53 colonels from the Air Force.

At Ling-Temco-Vought Aerospace Corporation, retired officers hold many jobs. Retired Air Force General G. P. Disosway is a vice president of the company. Former Rear Admiral Adrian H. Perry holds down the jobs of president of the Kentron Hawaii Ltd. subsidiary as well as vice president of LTV's Aerospace Corporation. Former Air Force Brigadier General H. G. Bench is listed as an assistant to the president of Ling-Temco-Vought itself. It is not unfair to think that these jobs and those of the 66 other generals, admirals, colonels, and Navy captains who work for LTV have some connection with the fact that LTV has almost a billion dollars of contracts with the Pentagon.

An examination of the former officers hired by this company, as well as by the others, shows that time after time they, like General Bench, retired one month (in his case, August, 1968) only to turn up on the company's payroll the next month (September, 1968).

From the detailed records the Pentagon finally provided, it was possible to examine the dates when many officers left their service jobs and went to work for one of the big military contractors. A typical example is the General Electric Company, which, in February, 1969, employed 89 former high-ranking officers. Of the 67 whose dates of retirement and dates hired by GE were tabulated by the Pentagon, 42, or almost 70 per cent, of them went to work for the company in six months or less after they retired. Four of the six flag officers hired by GE went with the company almost immediately. These included Brigadier General D. C. Lewis, who left the Army in July, 1962, and joined GE in November, as an "Army Consultant"; Marine Corps Major General W. R. Collins who retired in November, 1966, and was hired by GE in December as a "Military Planner"; and Air Force Brigadier General H. C. Huglin who retired in January, 1964, and joined the company as a "Senior Military Specialist" before the end of that month. Army Major General R. H. Adams waited for two months, from July to September, 1966, before he joined the company as manager of its Quality Assurance and Management Services. Air Force Brigadier General H. E. Neal waited eight months to join the company. Only former Rear Admiral W. T. Kinsella, who became manager of GE's Fleet Operational Data Project, spent more than a few months between retirement and the time he went to work for GE.

Not only were there more than 2,100 retired high-ranking officers employed by the 100 largest military contractors, at the time I asked for the records, but earlier records show also that the situation has been getting steadily worse, as time has gone on, and the military-industrial complex has grown stronger. Ten years before these details about the situation as of February, 1969, were made public, former Senator Paul H. Douglas had asked for, and received, a similar list from the Pentagon. His request was made in connection with hearings before the Senate Finance Committee on the 1959 extension of the Renegotiation Act. Thus, in spite of the Pentagon's reluctance to make public the data they receive every year from retired officers, we have these two benchmarks. Comparisons can therefore be made as to what happened during the decade.

In 1959, the total number of retired colonels or Navy captains and above who were employed by the 100 largest contractors—with 88 of those companies reporting—was 721. This was an average of slightly more than eight per company. In 1969, the figure was 2,124, or more than 21 per company.

In 1959, the ten companies with the largest number of former officers on their payrolls employed 372 of them. In 1969, the top ten had 1,065 or about three times as many as in 1959. In both years, the top ten employed almost precisely half of the total.

It was also possible to compare the 43 companies that were on the list and reported the facts in both 1959 and 1969. Additional companies were on the lists in both years, but failed to report the facts in one year or the other. These 43 companies together employed 588 high-ranking former officers in 1959. In 1969, they employed 1,642 high-ranking retired military officers.

In each case where a comparison can be made, the number has almost tripled. This is true of the total numbers employed in both years. It is true of the numbers employed by the top ten firms in both years. And, it is true of the numbers employed by firms that reported in both of those years.

Those are the facts. What is their significance? What do they mean? What are the implications of this situation? Is there anything to be learned from them? A great many people pooh-pooh them. Some have gone so far as to call their publication and the publication of the names of former officers a dastardly attack on the military. They have tried to wrap the flag around themselves and claim that disclosure of the truth comes close to an attack on our gallant fighting men.

But it was two famous ex-soldiers who gave the strongest warning against the influence of the military establishment. Not only did President Eisenhower, just as he was leaving office, warn against the danger of "unwarranted influence, whether sought or unsought, by the military-industrial complex," but George Washington in his Farewell Address also cautioned us against the military influence. The danger is now here. The 2,124 high-ranking former officers employed by the 100 biggest contractors constitute a major bulwark of that influence.

It is important to say exactly what that danger is. It is not a danger resulting from any conspiracy between the military and the 100 largest contractors. I do not claim or suggest such a thing.

The United States has been exceedingly fortunate in the calibre of its military leaders. The quality, high-mindedness, and faith in democracy shown by the nation's military leadership has been a hallmark of this country's history. Think of the great names of World War II—Marshall, Eisenhower, Nimitz, Bradley, Arnold, Spaatz, King—and of those men who gained fame after World War II—Hoyt S. Vandenberg, Maxwell Taylor, James Gavin, Lucius Clay, David M. Shoup, Wallace M. Greene, Lewis W. Walt, and William C. Westmoreland, to name only a handful.

Although it is true that a few military leaders, such as generals Mark Clark, Douglas MacArthur, Curtis LeMay, and Admiral Arleigh Burke held views far to the right, either they subordinated their political views while serving on active duty, or the President and the country, as in the instance of General MacArthur's insubordination, acted decisively to ensure civilian control. There has never been a rumor, let alone a scintilla of evidence, that the generals and admirals of recent times have conspired to take over the government by a military coup. For that we should be eternally grateful.

The officers now working for the big contractors include many who have performed valiant and even heroic service on behalf of the United States. The country is grateful to them for their patriotic accomplishments. We should eschew even the slightest suggestion of any conspiracy between the Pentagon, on the one hand, and the companies who hire former high-ranking officers, on the other. No evidence of any such conspiracy exists.

But what can be said, and should properly be said, and emphasized, is that there is a continuing community of interest between the military, on the one hand, and the companies who hire ex-officers, on the other.

These companies should be looked at just as the country looks at any other group of lobbyists. That is what they are. They are out to get big contracts for themselves. They promote within the law whatever supports their parochial interests. They organize to influence policy. They use influence and pressure to get things done in their own behalf. They organize letter-writing campaigns to congressmen and senators. Their officers make big campaign contributions. They have an impact on committee assignments in Congress. They fight over contracts and weapons systems. They pull strings to get favors and to avoid penalties.

Our failure is that, in the past, we have been unwilling to look upon the men in the military-industrial complex in these terms. Instead, we have confused national interest with their interests. The two are not the same.

Except for occasional instances, illegality or wrongdoing is not the major problem. Instead, what we have can be called the "old boy network." The employment of ex-officers by those who, in effect, wear the same old school tie, is a classic example of how the military-industrial complex really works. The revolving door through which officers and civilians shuttle back and forth between the Pentagon and the contractors is what the military-industrial complex is all about, and is a dangerous and shocking thing. The fact that 2,124 ex-officers are in the employ of the big contractors indicates the increasing influence of the contractors with the military and the military with the contractors. The increase in numbers over the last decade shows an intensification of the problem and the growing community of interest that exists between the two and makes it imperative that new weapons systems receive the most critical review and that defense contracts be examined in microscopic detail.

We should be alarmed not because the integrity or good will of most retired officers who work for the big contractors is in question, but, rather, we should be alarmed about the trend itself. It represents a distinct threat to the public interest. Because of its power and wealth, the military-industrial Establishment has an undue influence when decisions affecting the defense and foreign policies of this country are made. The views of the men in the military-industrial complex are by no means always wrong. But they do have a disproportionate influence on the decisions made by the executive branch of the government and by Congress. Instead of being one of many considerations taken into account, their influence has become the dominant factor. For many a courageous political figure in various areas of the government, it is difficult to vote or take other action against a proposed military project when the company that builds it is in his home state or district and thousands of men and women are employed there. For a congressman, not only the economic vitality of the district or state, but also his own political life may depend on his supporting the project even if its validity is questioned.

There are other reasons why the present situation is particularly dangerous. The lack of competition in bidding lends itself to major abuse. When only 11.5 per cent of military contracts are awarded on a formally advertised competitive bid basis, then influence, rather than the lowest responsible dollar bid, can, and often does, determine the outcome. When almost 90 per cent of all military contracts are negotiated and when a very high proportion of them are negotiated with only one or two contractors, the old school tie and the old boy network and who you know and what influence you have become the determining factors.

Former high-ranking military officers have an entree to the

Pentagon that others do not have. This is not necessarily wrong. But it is so, and it can and does lead to abuse. They have personal friendships with those still at the Pentagon, which most people do not have.

In some cases, former officers may be involved, at least indirectly, in negotiating contracts with their fellow officers still at the Pentagon. Or they are involved in proposing some of the thousands of change orders, which are one of the main reasons for the huge cost overruns on weapons system contracts. On the C-5A, there were three thousand of them, and they were obviously a factor in the escalation of its cost. Former officers may keep their skirts clean legally by avoiding direct negotiations on a contract to sell to their old service. But they may well be involved, and many are involved, in the change orders, which result in doubling or tripling the cost of contracts. There is little real difference between a former officer directly negotiating a million-dollar contract with the Pentagon, which may be illegal and prohibited, and an officer instituting change orders, which will raise the cost and fatten the pockets of the contractor by adding a million or more dollars to the total.

And what about those officers who are involved behind the scenes in making proposals, developing plans and specifications, drawing up blueprints, taking part in the planning process, or proposing prospective weapon systems? They may be doing these things in cooperation with their fellow officers with whom they have served and who, in some cases, they may even have promoted. With such a high proportion of negotiated contracts, there is a broad avenue for potentially dangerous abuse of the public interest.

The defenders of these practices always downgrade the criticism. But ask some simple questions. Why does Lockheed hire a retired admiral and a lieutenant general as its senior military advisers? Surely, the company is as interested in their contacts as in their ability. Why is Boeing's Washington representative a retired brigadier general? Was General Dynamics ignorant of General J. W. Kelly's influence when it hired him the same month he retired from the Air Force as the company's Washington international representative? Did it appoint Air Force Lieutenant General H. T. Alness to manage its office in the nation's capital on the altruistic grounds that retired lieutenant generals need post-retirement employment in order to put their kids through college? These men are hired for their contacts and their influence. Their value to a company is not due to their vast experience in business management or technical salesmanship.

There is something else wrong about present practices. This is the subtle and unconscious temptation to the officer still on active duty. He knows that over 2,000 of his fellow officers work for the big companies. He knows that under the promote-or-get-out policy of the military services he will retire at age fifty. Yet he has fifteen to twenty active years of life left. In the military, the outward manifestation of the trauma associated with this difficult period of transition in middle age is referred to as the "colonel's syndrome." There is much to be said for the officers who are forced to retire and much to be said against a system that throws them out at the peak of their careers.

But the point is this. How hard a bargain does an Air Force lieutenant colonel drive with Lockheed or Boeing or General Dynamics when he is representing the Air Force at one of their plants? He knows that shortly he will be forced to retire and that hundreds of his fellow officers work for these and other companies. Is he really going to bite the hand that may feed him? How hard is he going to buck the welfare system operating in the United States for the military-industrial establishment?

There have been direct instances of corruption or conflict of interest, but these are not the major problems. The true danger to the public interest is that the big defense firms and the former officers who work for them have a community of interest with the military itself. They hold a narrow view of public priorities based on self-interest. They have a largely uncritical view of military spending. They do not lack in good motives. The vast majority believe in what they are doing, just as any man must believe in what he is doing if he is to live with himself. Thus, they can and often do misjudge or exaggerate the need for a new expensive weapon.

Moreover, their narrow training re-enforces their prejudices. They may see only military answers to exceedingly complex diplomatic and political problems. A military response, or the ability to make one, may seem to them to be the most appropriate answer to every international threat.

The meaning of all of this is simple. The significance is there for everyone to see. When the bulk of the nation's budget goes for military purposes, when 100 companies get 68 per cent of the defense contract dollars, when cost overruns are routine, and prime military weapons system contracts normally exceed their estimates by 100 to 200 per cent, when these contracts are let by negotiation and not by competitive bidding, and when the top contractors have over 2,100 high-ranking retired military officers on their payrolls, the public interest is threatened. The warnings of Presidents Washington and Eisenhower must be taken seriously.

The response of the Department of Defense to such considerations strengthens my concern. After I made public the number of retired officers, their names, and the number employed by each of the top contractors, I received a detailed, five-page, single-spaced letter from Assistant Secretary of Defense for Installations and Logistics Barry Shillito, essentially defending the *status quo*. Some of his points were well taken. What alarmed me was his defensive attempt to justify all that has taken place.

He argued that the situation was not as bad as it seems, because the number of all retired officers working for the big contractors had gone up from 4.1 per cent of the total in 1959 to 5.6 per cent of the total in 1969. But this proves not only that the number has tripled but that the percentage has also gone up. Furthermore, far from being a comforting fact, 4.1 per cent was itself far too many and an increase to 5.6 per cent should be a cause for alarm.

He claimed that, because of company mergers and acquisitions, comparisons between the two years could not be accurate. Because of mergers and conglomerates, the 100 companies of 1959 are really 131 companies in 1969. That, of course, is true. But fundamentally, it does not affect the figures. In both years, the top ten companies employed almost half the total number of retired officers. The numbers employed by these ten companies almost tripled. The forty-three companies that were on both lists also showed the same pattern. Adding additional firms makes little difference to the total, since a relatively small number of firms employed most of the ex-officers. For example, the thirty-one firms employing the largest number of former officers—each had twenty or more on their payrolls—employed 83 per cent of all of them. The lowest sixty-nine had only 17 per cent.

Assistant Secretary Shillito made other points, too. He claimed that the retired officers made up only a very small proportion of the total employees of the firms. As the firms employed thousands, that is true. But it is equally true that, man for man, they were in much higher-paying and more important posts than the average employee. Their influence far outweighs their numbers. I am sure that none of them were hourly wage-earners in these plants of the giants.

It was also said that military officers retire at a much younger age than most civilian employees of the government. With children to educate and many productive years remaining, most officers must seek employment after retirement, it was argued, and one of the areas where they are most qualified to seek work is with the companies who produce military

hardware. That argument, to me, is upside down. The economic need on the part of high-ranking officers to go to work
for the big contractors is exaggerated. There are thousands of
other companies, where there is no conflict of interest what-
soever, plus teaching and public service jobs open to them.
No one can claim that they are hardship cases or that employment with the big companies is necessary for their survival.

The tone of the Pentagon's official reply was deeply dis-
turbing. The military services and DOD bureaucrats justify
what other men deplore. They defend the indefensible.
Secretary Shillito expressed his concern that "some may gain
the impression that there is an abnormal upsurge or serious
disproportionate growth in employment of retired officers in
this segment of our national economy." He concluded, "In
my view, the facts do not warrant those conclusions."

Public fears can only be fortified by such statements, ex-
pressing as they do the essential complacency of the Pentagon
in this and in other vital matters. But a cause for even greater
concern was the theme that ran through Secretary Shillitto's
letter: the view that the existing conflict-of-interest laws are
sufficient to prevent the appearance of, as well as actual, conflicts of interest.

"Don't worry," was his message. Even if 2,100 high-ranking
former officers work for the big contractors, the law prevents
any conflicts. Concerning these men, Secretary Shillito wrote:
"Their employment, as is the case of all of our approximately
700,000 retired military personnel, is covered by regulation
and laws which are designed to prevent conflict of interest."
And in a specific reference to those laws and the Defense Department regulations enforcing them, he stated, "We feel
these controls are sound and are working." But are they
sound? Are they working? During our Subcommittee's hearings on military procurement and national economic priorities, some disquieting testimony on conflicts of interest was
received from Merton Tyrrell, the vice president of the Performance Technology Corporation. PTC, as it is called, is a

firm of industrial efficiency experts. Before he began his job with the Air Force, A. E. Fitzgerald also worked for PTC.

The date was June 10, 1969. The witness: Merton Tyrrell. The general subject; the huge overrun on the Minuteman missile, the cost of which had soared from an estimated $3 billion to $7 billion. The specific subject: North American Rockwell's Autonetics subsidiary, which produced the guidance and control system for the Minuteman.

This was the colloquy:

SENATOR PROXMIRE. Mr. Tyrrell, this is one of the most shocking examples of waste and extravagance that I have seen in the years I have been in Washington. As I understand it, on Minuteman overall, we have been told by a witness before our committee last November, there was a profit of 42 per cent on invested capital. Now, in your statement you refer to the harmful effects as you put it "of the switchover of personnel between government and industry" the very thing Senator Goldwater and I were discussing, that is, procurement officials who go to work for the industry, and sometimes industry officials who come in and go to work in procurement. Can you explain what you mean specifically? How much of a problem was it on Minuteman? Let me put it this way. First, how many Defense Department officials, civilian or military, made the switch over to the contractor?

MR. TYRRELL. Well, in the area of the guidance and control area alone, there were a number of them. For example, the Air Force Plant Representative when we first arrived there, Colonel Rowland, retired and went to work for North American. Another Air Force Plant Representative while we were there, Colonel Yockey, retired and went to work for Autonetics.

SENATOR PROXMIRE. What jobs did these men hold in the Defense Department before they went to work?

MR. TYRRELL. They were the Air Force plant representative who was locally stationed at the contractor's plant and who in effect headed up the administration of the guidance and control contracts.

SENATOR PROXMIRE. Isn't there a law that prohibits a procurement official from going to work for the contractor with whom he is dealing within a period of two years?

MR. TYRRELL. I am not a lawyer, sir, and I could not tell you if there is a law to that effect.

SENATOR PROXMIRE. At any rate, you know as a matter of fact that these men did work on the Minuteman contract for the Air Force?

MR. TYRRELL. That is correct.

SENATOR PROXMIRE. And then went directly to work for the Minuteman contractor?

MR. TYRRELL. That is correct.

SENATOR PROXMIRE. What were their jobs with the contractor when they went to work for them?

MR. TYRRELL. Yockey I believe is a director of the business operations there. Major Klecker, who was the guidance and control project officer, is assistant program manager at Autonetics. I am not familiar with Colonel Rowland's title.

SENATOR PROXMIRE. Are there other people whose names you could give us?

MR. TYRRELL. Well, as I mentioned, Major Klecker, who was the project officer, went to work for Autonetics. Additionally, when we first arrived there there was a Colonel Richard Cathcart who subsequently retired and went to work for Autonetics. And he was the head of the BSD pricing before his retirement.

SENATOR PROXMIRE. In your judgment, is this prevalent in defense industry in its relationship with the Defense Department?

MR. TYRRELL. I think it is relatively prevalent. We see it quite frequently. And a number of personnel or military people do retire at a relatively early age, and they quite frequently go to work for the defense contractors.

SENATOR PROXMIRE. Is it your conviction that this is one of the reasons why there is a soft attitude toward cost overrun and why there isn't the kind of strict surveillance and discipline which you recommend?

MR. TYRRELL. I think it probably relates to that. I am not sure whether it is the sole cause. I think one of the things that tend to create the softness as you phrase it is the team concept that I brought out in my statement, wherein they consider themselves all members of the same team. And it becomes rather difficult, then, for them to disassociate themselves. And I don't think it is conscious collusion as was pointed out by the Senator, it is something that has just evolved. They are all part of the same group.

SENATOR PROXMIRE. Autonetics is a division of North American; is that correct?

MR. TYRRELL. Yes, it is.

In 1963, Performance Technology Corporation signed a contract with the Ballistics Systems Division of the Air Force. One of their first jobs was to review the guidance and control system for the Minuteman missile at North American's Autonetics Division.

The plant is located at Anaheim in Orange County, California, near Los Angeles and is composed of a series of one-story buildings with a high-rise executive suite. The company then employed about 30,000 people. Because of the acreage it covered and the huge parking lots surrounding it, locally it was referred to as "Disneyland East."

There the comparison stopped. Instead of an easy-going, fun-loving place, the plant was almost a caricature of Orwell's *1984* or Southern and Kubrick's *Dr. Strangelove*. Security was tight. Special identification badges were required. Almost weekly, the signal for a Big Brother–like sequence was

heard. Desk tops were cleaned; unfinished work stuffed in
the drawers. Then the doors swung open. Women dressed in
white smocks wheeled television receivers into the plant and
office rooms. A 10-minute, taped message combining a Vince
Lombardi–style pep talk with a Fourth of July oration came
over the tube. At the end, TV sets were rolled out, desk
drawers opened and the unfinished work retrieved and
stashed again on top of the desks.

When the PTC two-man team first arrived to check on the
company's efficiency for the Air Force, they were given an
office to work in, but were denied access both to the business
and production areas of the plant. Unable to retrieve company cost data directly or to check the production lines themselves, they made up lists of key documents they wanted. The
data were not produced. Company officials procrastinated.
Only bits and pieces were provided. Finally, the vice president of PTC forced the issue with the company and, in the
end, got sufficient information to begin making judgments.

It soon became clear from the company's own documents
that serious problems existed in the production of the PIGA's
(pendular integrating gyroscopic accelerometer). There were
special problems on its cost and reliability. The guidance
control system was functioning at less than half of the performance required by the specifications. To be effective at a
Minuteman missile site, the system had to run continuously.
The time between failures leading to removal and overhaul
of the missile's electronic brain was many hours short of what
it should have been. In addition, overhead costs at this very
early stage of the contract were already at a rate above those
planned and scheduled for the peak period of the five-year
term of work.

In sum, at the end of the first three months, it was plain
that there was a delay in the contract, reliability was half
what it should have been, and overhead costs were so excessive that a massive overrun was predicted.

Tyrrell, Fitzgerald, and PTC's team reported this to the Air Force. PTC proposed a cost reduction program to bring Autonetics in line with the target cost of the guidance system. The Air Force at the Systems Program Office in the Ballistics Systems Division at San Bernadino accepted their report. But, in the end, Air Force officials deleted all the recommendations relating to cost reduction. The best that can be said for their actions was that they were more interested in production than in reducing costs.

PTC continued its internal plant examination and again, in early 1964, projected a significant cost overrun. When the evidence was given to the company, the contractor agreed and even declared to the Air Force that the facts were correct. PTC again urged the implementation of its cost reduction program to the Systems Program Office.

Then, in the late spring of 1964, PTC was ordered to do a detailed cost study at Autonetics by the Ballistics System Division of the Air Force. When PTC experts arrived at Disneyland East, they got in to see the Air Force plant representative, Colonel Yockey. But even though they were there under an Air Force contract, Yockey denied them access to the plant. It took more than a month to work out that problem. Delays continued. Some information was never given. The final result was that no effective cost-cutting program as proposed by PTC was ever implemented.

In June, 1967, Ernie Fitzgerald stated, in a long memorandum to Air Force General J. W. O'Neill:

> In formulating a broad management improvement plan for Minuteman, I believe you should consider the problem posed by the mass migration of Air Force Officers into the management ranks of contractors with whom they have dealt.

Fitzgerald then cited his experience with the Autonetics Subsidiary of North American Rockwell, noting that the same Air Force plant representative "who revoked our clearances at Autonetics is now a division manager at Autonetics."

Fitzgerald's reference was to Colonel J. D. Yockey, who had prevented PTC's access to the Autonetics plant. In August, 1966, he retired from the Air Force and left his job as government representative at Autonetics. In September, 1966, he went to work for the company itself. In 1969, the Pentagon listed his job as "Director, Astrionics Operation" for North American Rockwell's aerospace and systems group.

Fitzgerald's memo to General O'Neill continued:

> His (Yockey's) predecessor, equally protective of the contractor's interest, is also now employed by North American Aviation.

This is a reference to Colonel Rowland, Yockey's predecessor as the Air Force plant representative at Disneyland East. Furthermore, Fitzgerald wrote:

> The procurement officer who blocked access by the Minuteman Program Control office to Autonetics contract negotiation records is now employed by North American Aviation.

Here, he is referring to Colonel Richard E. Cathcart. In 1963 and 1964, Cathcart was the Air Force project officer at Autonetics for guidance control—the man responsible for seeing that the government got a quality product at the estimated cost. Yet, he denied the experts from Performance Technology Corporation access to the Air Force negotiation files, which were crucial in determining the estimated overhead rates established for the project when the contract was negotiated.

According to Pentagon records, Colonel Cathcart retired from the Air Force in July, 1966, and went to work for North American Rockwell in August, 1966. His position is described as "Executive Planning Advisor."

Ernest Fitzgerald next referred to Major Klecker, the Air Force Project officer for guidance and control at the

Autonetics plant, stating, "The immediate superior of the project officer who was excluded from Autonetics plant is now employed by Autonetics."

Finally, Fitzgerald referred to former Lieutenant General W. A. Davis, who commanded the Ballistics System Division. The Air Force's Ballistics System Division originally contracted for the efficiency survey at the Autonetics plant. Over one-third of the report made by Fitzgerald and Tyrell to the Ballistics System Division urged a cost reduction program at Autonetics to bring the costs in line with the original target costs. The Air Force accepted the PTC proposal, but deleted all the specific tasks in it related to cost reduction. In fact, no effective program was ever carried out.

In his memo, Fitzgerald, referring to this incident and to General Davis, writes, "The officer cited to me as responsible for killing the cost reduction project I contracted to perform at Autonetics is now employed by North American Aviation."

Following his Air Force assignment with the Ballistics System Division, General Davis became the Vice Commander of the Air Force Systems Command located at Andrews Air Force Base just outside Washington, D.C. In May, 1967, according to the Pentagon documents, he joined North American Rockwell as a group vice president. In what has the appearance of an error, the Pentagon states that he did not retire until two months later in July, 1967. (This may be accounted for if General Davis went to work for the company before he used up his terminal leave. In any event, according to the Pentagon records as they stand, he went to work for North American even before he left the Air Force.)

Later, I referred this testimony to the Department of Justice. I did so in part because of the repeated Pentagon assurances that the employment of retired officers was covered "by regulations and laws which are designed to prevent conflict of interest."

Secretary Shillito had written, "We feel these controls are sound and are working." But these government contracting officers and plant representatives left the government and went to work for the company where they had been representing the government on contracts with that company. In such cases, there certainly appears to be a *prima facie* case of a serious conflict of interest.

The Air Force hired efficiency experts to examine Autonetics costs and procedures. Yet, Air Force officers at the plant refused them access both to the plant and to contract negotiating information needed to carry out their work.

"If this is not a conflict of interest," I wrote to the Attorney General, "then the laws and the Department of Defense directives are not worth the paper they are written on."

Ernest Fitzgerald summed it up in his memorandum to General O'Neill. "Lest you accuse me of being unfair to North American and the officers they have employed, I concede that the condition I have described is not unique. Indeed, it is common enough to be our next national scandal."

VIII

How Tall Is the Adversary?

ON JULY 9, 1969, when the Senate was debating the authorization for military procurement, research, and deployment, a number of questions were raised: on the ABM, on Pentagon-financed research, etc. The ensuing discussions were useful and valuable. They highlighted technical and policy problems of the most serious nature. But to my mind, at any rate, the debate focused on the wrong issues. The right issue was defined by Senator Henry M. Jackson, of the state of Washington, in his speech on the Senate floor. He said:

> The central issue which you have to decide first, before you decide what kind of military budget you should have or what kind of foreign policy you should have, is, what kind of adversary do you face, and what is he up to?

I disagreed, to some extent, with Senator Jackson's conclusions in that speech. But, in the sentence quoted, he put his finger on what, in my view, is absolutely crucial. To reach sound judgments on the size and composition of our own military budget, we must understand not only the nature of the Soviet challenge, but we must also have an accurate evaluation of the Soviet capability. This, in turn, calls for an accurate and objective appraisal of the Soviet economy.

Does the Soviet economy permit Russia to mount a military challenge to the United States? What kind of a challenge? How protracted could it be?

In addition, we need an accurate assessment of the temper of the Soviet people. What are their priorities? To what extent does the Soviet Government make an effort to satisfy those priorities? The answers to these questions have a direct bearing on the Soviet military potential, and, consequently, on expenditures for national defense by the United States.

The committee of the Senate that should be most directly concerned with this problem, the Armed Services Committee, has not solicited any information on this subject. When it was considering the defense authorization, no testimony of any kind was offered before the Armed Services Committee on the basic economic capability of the Soviet Union and its relation to any military challenge.

Such estimates should be contained in the Secretary of Defense's annual posture statement. But the posture statement essentially eschews an analysis of the Soviet economy and presents an analysis based almost exclusively on the quantity and quality of Soviet weapons and the threat they potentially pose.

When, as Chairman of the Subcommittee on Economy in Government, I decided that we should be concerned with the American military budget because of its impact on the economy, my intent was to try to fill a serious information gap. We devoted three weeks of Subcommittee hearings to an intensive review of that budget, in the context of over-all national priorities. In the course of those hearings, it was apparent that the actual or potential threat of the Soviet Union to the United States, and, indeed, to the world, is the dominant factor in our military planning. Hence, we decided to include intensive hearings on the Russian economy and its military potential.

It is obvious that our estimate of the Soviet military capability is the decisive element in determining our own military budget requests. The funds available for domestic needs are, thus, directly related to our evaluation of the Soviet scene. The allocation of priorities within the United States, in short, depends upon our assessment of the priorities within the Soviet Union.

There is a school of thought which holds that the Soviet dictatorship does not really have to worry about priorities. This school argues that the Soviet hierarchy is so powerful that it can simply commandeer and allocate resources to accomplish whatever goal it sets for itself at a given time. According to this view, if the Soviet Union desires to attain military supremacy over the United States, for example, it can marshal the resources necessary to attain that goal. If the Soviet people suffer in the process, well, that is the nature of totalitarianism.

One does not have to be a specialist in Soviet affairs to realize that this view is oversimplified. Soviet political forces do shape Soviet decisions on the allocation of resources. But we need to know whether the Russians have stepped up their military forces and armaments and, if so, by how much? What price do they then pay in terms of educational cutbacks or the postponement of planned expansion of their capital base? In the long run, what happens in these categories means greater or less efficiency and greater or smaller output. In the long run, the Soviet Union cannot stunt education or capital investment without weakening its military strength.

We were also interested in probing such matters as the influence of the Soviet military, the possibilities of organizing dissent, and the implications of the Czech invasion and the border clashes with China.

Admittedly, these considerations were general. But our Subcommittee felt that a general discussion would be useful to it, Congress, the executive branch of government, and the people. We felt that it would be particularly relevant to our analysis of the U.S. military budget to have a firmer grasp of the political and economic forces shaping Soviet decision-making at the present time. For that purpose, we held hearings on June 23 and 24, 1969, entitled "The Economic Basis of the Russian Military Challenge to the United States." Our witnesses were professors Merle Fainsod, Alex Inkeles, and Abram Bergson, of Harvard, Joseph Berliner, of Brandeis, Holland Hunter, of Haverford College, William Kintner, of the University of Pennsylvania, Dr. Thomas Wolfe, of the RAND Corporation, and David E. Mark, of the State Department.

These men, the leading American experts on the Soviet Union and its economic potential, represented a reasonably diverse range of opinion on Soviet military and economic strength. The conclusions that follow, drawn from their testimony and informed by their expertise, give us a realistic basis on which to view the Soviet threat.

The first and, perhaps, the most fundamental conclusion about the Soviet economy and its ability to support a military establishment is that, although Russia has about 10 per cent more population than the United States, its economy is only half the size of ours. The total amount that the Soviet Union expends on defense is estimated at about 20 billion rubles. This converts roughly to 22 billion dollars. A quick glance at that figure makes it seem as if the Soviet military budget is about one-quarter of our own. But, one cannot make a simple monetary comparison. Prices and wages in the United States and the Soviet Union are not comparable. If price and wage differentials are taken into account, Soviet expenditures for defense rise to an amount variously estimated from 40 to 50 billion dollars.

The Institute of Strategic Studies, in London, estimates the military budget of the Soviet Union at the lower figure. On that basis, Soviet military spending, with an economy only half as productive as ours, is roughly proportionate to that of the United States. With a gross national product one-half the amount of ours, they spend one-half as much on their military establishment as we do on our military establishment.

The percentage of its gross national product that the Soviet Union spends on defense is also roughly comparable to ours. Most of the estimates given our Subcommittee set the current percentage at around 9 to 10 per cent.

There is, of course, a hidden aspect to Soviet military expenditures that does not come out in published appropriation figures. Soviet military-related expenditures, such as those for research and development, and internal security, are hidden elsewhere in Soviet accounts. They are not given under military outlays.

Of course, one can argue that the U.S. Central Intelligence Agency expenses do not show up in the U.S. military budget either, or at least where they can be identified. Expenditures for nuclear warheads appear in the Atomic Energy Commission budget and not in the Department of Defense budget. But American research and development is quite openly identified. And, although certain expenses for internal security or nuclear warheads are not carried as military requests in our budget, they are nonetheless counted in the total. Also, we do not maintain a security police or a border guard that is militarized to the extent that these forces are militarized in the Soviet Union. Consequently, our unidentified amounts are relatively smaller.

Even when allowances have been made for hidden costs,

however, the percentage of the total Soviet output devoted to the military is in the same order of magnitude as the published budgetary figures. For example, one of the witnesses, Professor Hunter, noted that the upper limit of Soviet defense spending was about 10 per cent of the gross national product, and this included hidden defense-related outlays. Dr. Wolfe, of the RAND Corporation, said the range was 10 to 15 per cent. This figure included concealed expenditures. These differences do not seem highly significant.

Similarly, estimates of military manpower vary, depending upon whether one includes paramilitary forces or not. It appears fair to say that at an approximate strength of 3 million men, the Soviet armed forces actually contain about half a million less than our own. If one wishes to include the security police and the border guards in the calculation, then the Soviet manpower commitment appears to be slightly larger than our own. This latter was the view of the RAND spokesman, but it is not one that all observers consider proved.

Given its troubles with Communist China, its problems with restive regimes in Eastern Europe, and the possibility that, under the Brezhnev Doctrine, it may intervene elsewhere, one has to expect that the Soviet Union will maintain a very substantial military establishment. Indeed, if the thesis of several of the witnesses is correct, namely, that the Soviet military budget and the Soviet military effort has been based primarily on what the United States does, then, Soviet military manpower will continue to correspond roughly to ours.

We know that the Soviet Union can mount and maintain a major military effort. Indeed, it can sustain an immense military effort for some time, particularly if it is attacked or invaded, and the patriotic spirit of its people is aroused, as it was in World War II. We know that the present Soviet leadership conducts defense policy according to a philosophy embodied in Premier Alexei Kosygin's statement that "to economize on defense would be acting against the interests of the Soviet state and the Soviet people."

Finally, we know, as Professor Bergson put it, that the "Soviet Government has been seeking to support a military establishment of the first class with an economy that by U.S. standards has been of the second class." Still, he concluded, "the Government has found the necessary means so far, and it should be able to continue to do so."

Professor Hunter reached the conclusion that "Soviet military power now exists on the basis of a share of national output that has been small enough to be accompanied by rapid economic growth and rising living standards."

In this situation, some would argue that there are limited prospects for a reduction in the Soviet military establishment. Yet other very important factors in the Soviet economy may well act as a brake on military ambitions. For example, there are social aspirations, a phrase Professor Fainsod used, that are in conflict with military priorities. There is obviously a mutual U.S.–U.S.S.R. interest in defusing the arms race and reducing military expenditures, although there has been little progress toward that goal, and negotiations will probably be long and tedious.

The Achilles heel of the Soviet economy is obviously in agriculture. In their more than fifty years in power, the Communists have never solved that problem. At present, Russia, compared proportionally to the United States, devotes seven times more of its population to agriculture. Yet, it produces 20 per cent less food. This immense levy on manpower is a distinct drag on the Soviet economy. Manpower that might otherwise be used more productively is simply chewed up by inefficient agriculture.

The Russians could work their way out of this morass if they provided incentives and allocated more resources to fertilizer production, irrigation, and manufacture of agricultural machinery. If Soviet agriculture does not become more mechanized, there will not be a significant reduction in the manpower devoted to agriculture. But, if more of their limited resources are devoted to improving agriculture, those devoted to the military will have to be cut.

In addition, the inefficiency of agriculture is compounded by the manpower pinch elsewhere. Senator Allen J. Ellender, who visits Russia quite frequently, reported that he noted, in a plant manufacturing harvesters in Rostov-on-the-Don, that the harvesters being produced were of a heavy and inefficient old style. When he asked why the quality of the harvesters was not higher, he was informed that to improve production would mean retooling. This, in turn, would require additional skilled personnel, who were not available, to do the retooling job. So, this factory wastefully continued to manufacture inefficient machinery. Of course, to retool agriculture equipment would also take resources away from the military.

The implications of this agricultural failure bulk large for the rest of the Soviet economy. Thirty million productive workers have to toil in the fields and cannot be released for work in other sectors of the economy. Thus, the entire economy is weakened, and, with it, the Soviet military potential. Moreover, along with its difficulties in agriculture, the Soviet Union's military programs are limited by the nation's desire for continuing economic growth. In its intense urge to overtake and surpass the United States, it must choose between economic growth and military spending. To maintain a growth rate that would accomplish their economic objective, the Russians have had to maintain an extremely high rate of domestic investment. And Soviet economic growth has been very expensive in terms of the amount of additional capital required. Even in the heyday of Soviet growth, in the 1950's, the rapid growth in output was achieved only through a decidedly more rapid growth of capital.

According to Professor Bergson, over the decade 1950–60,

the stock of Soviet capital per unit of output grew 22 per cent. By 1965, an interval half as long, it had grown another 14 per cent. The almost inescapable conclusion is that the Soviet Government must be plowing back an ever-increasing share of output into new investment. This reinvestment, again according to Professor Bergson, is necessary not to raise the tempo of growth but merely to maintain it.

It is one of the ironies of our time that the Soviet growth rate has declined, despite this heavy capital investment, from a rate exceeding 7 per cent during 1950–58, to an average of 5.5 per cent for the years 1962–67, and that, while the Soviet growth rate was declining, the U.S. rate was rising. As matters stand, Soviet prospects for significantly narrowing the U.S. advantage are poor. The Soviet concern with lagging economic progress has been evidenced by its vigorous search for new forms of economic organization. It is apparent that more than just ever increasing investment will be necessary if the Soviet Union is to use technological progress for economic growth in the same degree as the United States.

Again, all of this has an obvious bearing on the Soviet military posture. For, if the Russians place their priorities on a stronger military establishment, they must, perforce, take resources from industrial development. This means that over-all economic growth will further slow down. In short, if the Russians take this option, their fundamental capacity to provide military hardware and support will suffer.

One might say, then, that the process of expanding Soviet military forces is self-limiting. Obviously, there are economic limits to the expansion of U.S. forces too. But, with a national income twice that of the Soviet Union, our limit would be reached at a much later time.

In the long run, resources poured into the military tend to limit a nation's fundamental military capacity. Only those funds and investments that greatly broaden the base of an economy ultimately strengthen that economy. This important aspect of the Russian military capacity is essentially overlooked in the annual posture statement presented by the Secretary of Defense to Congress.

There are obviously pressing problems facing the United States today, problems of primary importance to our national security, if broadly defined. The nation's security is adversely affected when millions of its citizens are living in poverty, when their education is inferior, or when they are prey to crime or injustice. Most of all, real security is affected if citizens lose faith in their government's willingness or capacity to do anything about these problems.

The United States must also make choices. Our problems make claims on the allocation of our resources and can reduce those that go to the military. The military budget is being cut back, however grudgingly. Congress is examining the Pentagon's requests with a considerably more critical eye than in the past. The shameless cover-up of cost overruns and the wasteful excesses of the military-industrial complex have devalued the Pentagon's credibility. Because of the unpopularity of the Vietnam War, the continued bad advice from the Joint Chiefs of Staff, and the unpopularity of high taxes and the draft, it is entirely conceivable that our military spending will be cut back sooner, and, to a much greater degree, than would be indicated by the simple, but crucial, fact that our gross national product is twice that of the Soviet Union.

A similar situation could obtain in the Soviet Union, where the pent-up demand for consumer goods is, in its own way, analagous to the demands in the United States for meeting our pressing domestic needs and reducing their attendant evils. The easy assumption is that the order of magnitude is not comparable. Large sums will be needed if we are to meet the urgent problems of our society. Some argue that the sums the Russians might have to allocate to plug the gap in consumer goods would be on a smaller scale. Some believe it would be so much less as not to be comparable.

But, as Professor Inkeles pointed out, that may well not be the case at all. For one cannot escape the fact that, despite a U.S. outlay on defense that is twice that of the Russians, the standard of living in this country is still far out of reach for all but a very few Soviet citizens. From the standpoint of producing consumer goods, it may not be an exaggeration to argue that the Soviet Union is an underdeveloped country. Certainly, it is grossly inefficient. Therefore, the effort that Russia might have to make to satisfy its people's need for a better living standard might well be comparable and, perhaps, even relatively greater than the effort the United States will have to make to cope with the unfulfilled needs of our society. If the Russians continue to pour into the military effort vast resources that are needed elsewhere, in the long run, their military effort will be hampered both by a lack of an adequate industrial base and a failure to meet the legitimate demands of their citizens. This probability cannot be emphasized too strongly.

The central issue is this: How strong is the demand for more and better consumer goods in the Soviet Union, and what is the Soviet Government prepared to do about it? Can it ignore these demands?

A glib answer, and one that might be true under extreme stress, is that it really doesn't make any difference—that consumer demand is irrelevant to Soviet planning. Yet, if one probes any distance beneath the surface, it becomes apparent that the governing apparatus of the Soviet Union is compelled to pay heed to consumer grievances. For the Russian worker, like any other worker, must have an incentive, and he must have some rewards. This is an economic fact of life that has long been recognized within the Soviet Union.

The Soviet worker wants improved consumer goods. He

wants better food. Certainly, he desires better housing. The longer the improvement in the consumer-goods picture is deferred, the more the worker becomes disinterested, the weaker his drive or willingness to work, and the less useful he is as a member of the Soviet economy and society.

Russia under Stalin followed the course of building up investment at the price of consumption. The price paid in human terms was excessive. On the whole, the policy was self-defeating. And, according to expert testimony before the Joint Economic Committee, China under Mao followed the same policy with the same disadvantages to efficiency and initiative.

From time to time in recent years, the Soviet Union has been able to shift a part of its resources to consumer goods. Positive results were immediately felt in the field of industrial production. There was increased efficiency and a higher rate of growth. All of this was achieved not because the Soviet Union set a national goal of feeding and housing people better, but because it correctly assumed that a better-fed and better-housed people was more productive. If, at this juncture, the Soviet Union should choose to cut back on consumer goods in order to funnel more resources into the military, productive efficiency, in my view, would surely and certainly decline again. This, in turn, would affect the efficiency of the military. While appearing to do more, because more resources would be going to the military and less to the society for its consumption or investment needs, the Russians might actually be doing less. In other words, short-run military strengths become long-run weaknesses.

It is because the Soviet leadership is aware of the importance of incentives, and is desirous of increasing output, that the ordinary Soviet citizen has some leverage today. As Professor Fainsod put it:

Even at the base of the Soviet social pyramid, rank and file, peasants and workers are now in a position to exert greater influence on the course of elite decision-making. When collective or state farm workers respond to inadequate incentives by listless performance in the public sector, by transferring their energies to private plots, or by abandoning their jobs to seek better paid work in the industrial centers, they in effect bargain to improve their position. They vote with their feet. In the absence of large-scale terror, there is a point beyond which they cannot be driven. If more production is to be extracted from them, improved incentives have to be provided. The state and party functionaries responsible for increasing agricultural output find themselves forced to plead the case of their peasant clients. In a perhaps perverted form, what takes place is a form of direct representation.

What is true for the peasant and the agricultural worker is equally true for those who work in Soviet industry. Professor Fainsod continued:

The same principle applies more or less to the industrial worker. In the absence of forced labor, workers abandon unattractive jobs in search of better opportunities. Those who are responsible for the recruitment of labor in difficult circumstances—whether they be enterprise directors or party secretaries—recognize that they must provide incentives or amenities if they are to attract a work force. Willingly or unwillingly, they become spokesmen for the workers' needs and aspirations when they argue the case for greater incentives as a key to increased production.

One might say that, in a limited way, there is a form of group representation operating in Soviet Russia. The Russian political order today is certainly not pluralist, but the party cannot be indifferent to the aspirations of the technical and professional people, the industrial workers, or the farm workers. It cannot remain indifferent, that is, if it desires continued economic and technological progress. Of course, it has the alternative of returning to mass terror, but that would appear to be self-destructive. Under present conditions, based on the assumption that the Soviet Union desires to increase productivity, it must increase the production of consumer goods.

If I may digress a moment, the military tends to act alike the world over. The activity of generals is not without its wry humor. When the Soviet defense budget was reduced in 1965, the Soviet military leaders, like their counterparts in this country, conducted what was, in effect, a lobbying campaign against the cut. They lacked the profusion of mass media, the imaginative use of advertising that is a feature of our own lobbying campaigns, and the vast network of public relations specialists found in the Pentagon. Consequently, they confined themselves to the columns of *Red Star,* the official journal of the Soviet armed forces. But the burden of their argument had a familiar ring. The military budget could not be cut. The country should err only on the side of more defense. Change the type face and the reports of their remarks could be substituted for testimony before the Armed Services Committees or an editorial in one of the American military journals.

There are further points. Soviet man does not live by bread alone. Scientists, writers, and artists presumably need incentives other than creature comforts. Those intellectuals who conform and act as the custodians and articulators of Communist Party orthodoxy, are among the most favored citizens of the Soviet Union. Those of the intelligentsia who have the temerity to question the basis of the system are quickly dispatched, either to jail, to mental institutions, or to forced labor camps, or their views are effectively banned in some other way. The voices of dissent, genuine dissent, in the Soviet Union are few and far between and are usually silenced more swiftly and efficiently than were the dissenters in Czarist days. In short, although sympathy for some of the ideas of the dissenters may exist in the ranks of Soviet intellectuals, few will risk overt opposition to the regime. What sentiment may exist for greater intellectual freedom does not constitute any real constraint on the government in its policy decisions, whether in domestic affairs, or in foreign or military policy.

What do these pros and cons, strengthens and weaknesses, all add up to in terms of U.S.–U.S.S.R. relations? What will be their effect on chances for *détente;* what prospects are offered for arms limitation?

One answer is that real Soviet needs, as well as some internal measures, offer genuine prospects for arms limitation, and, thereby, enhance the possibilities of a broader *détente.* The inescapable conclusion one draws, after examining the situation in any depth, is that both the United States and the Soviet Union should have a strong interest in a moratorium on anti-missile systems and offensive weapons. The problem is to confirm that mutual interest by meaningful agreements. When dealing with the Soviet Union, identifying a mutual interest is one thing; negotiating a binding instrument on the basis of such interests is likely to be something far more difficult and arduous.

While the Soviet leaders confront the United States in the military field (and, as former Secretary of State Dean Acheson has pointed out to our Subcommittee, confrontation and negotiation go hand in hand in the Soviet view), they must know that even their best efforts to build superior military power can be met and matched by this country with a smaller relative sacrifice. Russia may go all out to build the biggest and most threatening navy, air force, and missile force of which it is capable by 1975, sacrificing consumer goods, industrial investment, and agriculture in the process. Yet the end result would be a weaker economy, a Russian worker poorly motivated and, perhaps, dangerously alienated, an even greater lag behind the West in capital equipment, and an agriculture that continues to absorb nearly a quarter of productive Soviet manpower.

The Soviet leadership may be insecure, and it may be un-imaginative. It may even be stupid. But I do not think it is that stupid.

Whatever the failings of the Soviet leadership may be, the Russians have the advantage over us of knowing what we are up to, because ours is an open society, whereas, to obtain information about the Soviet Union, we must pore over documents, spend large amounts of time and money on analysis, and, possibly, employ clandestine means. The Russians, while maintaining their own clandestine establishment for information-gathering, need only read our newspapers to obtain great amounts of significant—and insignificant—information about us. They are omnivorous readers. And they read not only our newspapers, but our technical, scientific, and military journals as well. The Soviet leaders know that whatever they do to augment their military capability, we can more than meet it. If need be, we can double their effort, plane for plane, missile for missile, rifle for rifle. If they choose to enter an arms race with us, economically, it will be a losing proposition for them. This they know.

Logically, therefore, the Soviet Union should have every reason to want to enter an arms agreement with the United States. Assuming an agreement was reached that could be enforced by unilateral inspection—for example, air surveillance—the Soviet Union would have the opportunity to build its consumer-goods production, add to its industrial plant, and improve its agriculture in a balanced way. This would increase its over-all strength. And an increase in basic over-all strength means an increase in ultimate military potential. Furthermore, such an agreement could help the Russians maintain their superiority over the Chinese—an absolute superiority that might decline if the nonmilitary sectors were to be starved for a number of years. It could also mean a strengthened economic position *vis-à-vis* the Eastern European Communist countries.

Economic deterioration could increase Soviet insecurity and might tempt the Russians to new Czechoslovakia-style invasions. Conversely, heightened economic strength could lead to genuine Soviet security, which might, in time, in the words of Winston Churchill, allow fresh breezes to blow.

No claim is made that the Soviet Union is desperate for an arms control agreement. Obviously, it is not. But, pressing national needs make it highly likely that the Russians are seriously interested.

If one takes a skeptical view toward Soviet power and intentions, a view which does not underrate the Soviet Union or its capacity, it seems clear that there are many areas of U.S. military programing that can safely be reduced, without any loss to our national security. But it is vital that we continue the negotiations with the Soviet Union on strategic arms control—the SALT talks.

I think that a clear, hard look at the Soviet posture reveals that there is no necessity for this country to duplicate and exceed every Soviet initiative in terms of individual weapons systems.

We have four times the long-range bomber strength of the Soviet Union. We have fifteen attack carriers, each carrying many attack aircraft and surrounded by a fleet of escort vessels. Each of these sea-fortress complexes costs approximately $1.8 billion. The Soviet Union has none—not a carrier. The Russians have certain things we do not. They have an embryonic ABM system. We are about to get one, although the need for it is highly debatable, to say the least. Their elementary ABM poses no major problem of penetration. We have a great many more missiles than do they, although some of the individual Soviet missiles may carry greater megatonnage. All of this means that we can destroy each other.

We do have far greater economic leeway than the Soviet Union.

The Russians are not ten feet tall. Their economic capacity is half that of ours. Their military expenditures are also roughly in that proportion. If they overspend in the military field, they weaken their industrial capacity, their economic might, and their military potential. These facts, not some annual alarming statement from the Defense Department or the Joint Chiefs of Staff, should determine our basic military effort.

We have the economic and military capacity not only to meet their immediate threat but any foreseeable threat. The fact that we have double their economic and military strength may not keep them from making a miscalculation. But it is sufficient to keep us militarily safe and economically strong.

This is not an argument that there is no military threat from the Soviet Union. Those who witnessed postwar pressures on Berlin, who recall the rape of Hungary and Czechoslovakia, and who remember how the Red Army's presence in Eastern Europe snuffed out freedom there, could not fail to learn the lessons of history.

The sole issue is the size of the military establishment we need to meet this very real threat. And the conclusion is surely that a military expenditure that is double that of the Soviet Union is adequate to meet any immediate threat and to provide sufficient security against future threats without our reacting hysterically to every change in Soviet weapon manufacture or military strategy. There is no need to rush headlong into the expenditure of billions of dollars every time the Soviet Union launches a helicopter carrier or erects an anti-aircraft station in the suburbs of Moscow. We need not anticipate the threat of a new weapon that does not exist merely on the grounds that the Russians have the ultimate capability to deploy it.

The fact is that if we are figuratively six feet tall, the Russians are not ten feet, but only three feet tall.

What can be said of the Russian threat can be said many times over of the Chinese Communist threat. Let there be no misunderstanding of my meaning. No one should underrate the aggressiveness of the Red Chinese. No one should be fooled into thinking they are liberal reformers. Their threat, their bombast, and their intentions must not be discounted.

But the main questions are what real threat do they pose and how large a defense establishment do we need to meet it? The answer to the first is that their basic military threat is no greater than can be sustained by their fundamental economic position. And, in truth, their economic strength, their industrial capacity, their agricultural productivity, and the skill of their labor force are so limited that their fundamental military threat is exceedingly small. But this does not mean that they will act rationally. They may well take rash and foolish steps. To meet their threat, however, and to answer the second of the above questions, we do not need a military capacity ten, twenty, or one hundred times the size of theirs.

Unfortunately, as far as the basic Chinese military threat is concerned, we have made very large unneeded expenditures. This country has devoted a great deal of its enormous military spending to combating the expansion of Communist China. In Vietnam, for example, perhaps the major reason for our immensely expensive involvement has been to stop Communist expansion. The government's strong commitment in Vietnam has been characterized as based on the notion that our active military presence constitutes the cork in the bottle that contains Communist expansion. There may be some truth to this.

But Vietnam is only part of our military effort to contain Red China. This effort also includes our many heavily manned far-Pacific bases, our costly aircraft carriers, the other components of our Far Eastern fleets and their reserves, as well as a major Air Force commitment. The reason for all this is the fear that, without a vigorous and active military presence, Red China would sweep throughout Asia and, perhaps, extend far beyond.

This is probably the most expensive illusion of our time.

What kind of a threat does mainland China really constitute to the United States? How seriously do the Communist Chinese threaten our national interests in Asia? Could China execute a successful invasion well beyond its own borders on the Asian land mass? Could it mount a serious attack in the Pacific?

Consider the facts: In spite of vigorous, sometimes vicious, denunciation by Red China of U.S. involvement in Vietnam, at the time of this writing there has been no verified report of a single Chinese soldier involved in the Vietnam War. Why? Surely not because of any moral or peaceful compunction on the part of the Chinese. It is due largely to the fact that China does not have the economic strength to support any large military effort except on its immediate borders. China lacks transportation facilities. It has no navy worth of the name. It has a pitifully inadequate air force. Its highway system, rail system, and rolling stock are barely adequate to provide border protection.

Within the borders of China, the 750 million inhabitants, widely equipped with small arms, would constitute a highly formidable, probably an impossible force to overcome unless the use of massive nuclear arms were resorted to. But a possible world-conqueror Red China is not. It does have a nuclear arsenal, but it is primitive compared to that of the United States and Russia.

Most significant of all, China has not been gaining economic strength. It has been losing it.

A few years ago, the Joint Economic Committee conducted an intensive study of the economy of China. We commissioned twenty leading world scholars to do the job. The study showed a zigzag course of progress and setback for the Chinese economy.

Without a strong and growing economy, the Chinese threat dissolves in smoke. And the most recent reports, as the Chinese Communists celebrate their twentieth year in power, show how unlikely it is that China will constitute a serious threat in coming years. The Maoists face their third decade with massive problems and handicaps. Theirs is the only major country in the world that has not grown economically in the past ten years. China's gross national product of $75 to $80 billion is probably no higher than it was a decade ago. But China has annual population growth of 15 to 20 million, which has destroyed attempts to raise the standard of living or the military power, except for a rudimentary nuclear strength. Moreover, China's dangerous dispute with the Soviet Union over borders and ideological influences and its continued hostility toward not only the United States but most other countries add to the country's strains and uncertainties.

Certainly, the United States, along with other Pacific powers, should maintain a constructive military presence in the Pacific, but we are spending far more than can possibly be justified now.

The only justification for our enormous military expenditures lies in the threat of potential enemies. Two nations have seemed to constitute the overwhelming basis for this threat: the Soviet Union and the mainland Chinese. Both are limited militarily by economic constraints. As we have seen, the Soviet Union spends about half as much on its military operations as the United States. It has half the gross national product. It is constrained by an industry and agriculture that simply cannot afford to give up resources in favor of immediate military needs without seriously weakening its long-term economic, and, hence, military, power.

But, in Red China, we confront a far more conspicuously overestimated adversary. Our gross national product is $950 billion, or twelve times their $75 to $80 billion. On a per capita basis, it is about fifty times their gross national product.

If we are figuratively six feet tall and the Russians three feet tall, the Chinese are not ten feet but only six inches tall.

The cost of this overestimate to the American people in military overspending, in inflation, in an onerous tax burden, in shamefully inadequate housing, and in a series of other neglected domestic problems is very great indeed.

IX

Future Megatonnage:
Action and Reaction

THE PETERKINS were a large, closely knit, but not very bright family. To keep the household organized was no mean trick. With the Peterkins, survival itself was an achievement. The fact is they were blunderers.

I like to tell a story about them, adapted from the first chapter of Lucretia P. Hale's *The Peterkin Papers.*

One morning at breakfast, somebody poured too much sugar into the huge pot of coffee brewed for the clan. It was so sweet that none could stand its sickening taste. Then somebody else suggested that the way to offset the sweetness was to add equal quantities of salt. The salt made the coffee taste worse. New quantities of sugar were called for. Alternately, sugar and salt were poured into the mix—but to no avail. It was either too sweet or too salty.

In desperation, the Peterkin family resorted to chanting incantations over the steaming mess. But this ritual sorcery did not work.

At their wits' end, the Peterkin clan finally turned for advice to the Lady from Philadelphia, who was known for her great sagacity.

"What shall we do?" the Peterkins cried.

"The answer is simple," the Lady from Philadelphia replied. "Throw it out and start all over."

What happened to the Peterkins' coffee is not unlike what has happened to the world in the arms race.

When word was first gathered by U.S. intelligence forces that the Russians were to deploy their Tallinn anti-aircraft defense, we wrongly judged that this anti-aircraft defense for Moscow would soon be converted into a limited anti-ballistic-missile defense system and that Russia had the capability to deploy it in other cities, too. That, we believed, would reduce the effectiveness of our ICBM force. Consequently, we proceeded to deploy the Poseidon missile with its multiple warheads on our nuclear submarines. Eventually, we may have 31 submarines, each with 16 missiles carrying 10 to 14 warheads apiece, or almost 5,000 "hard target killers."

A Tallinn anti-ballistic-missile system, against which the Poseidon missiles were ordered deployed, never materialized. The Tallinn is and never was anything more than a straight anti-aircraft defense. But, when that became known, we did not stop the Poseidon program. It was continued as a hedge against a faster-than-expected deployment by the Soviet Union of the huge SS-9 missiles.

That was not all. As the Russians had the capability to deploy the SS-9 faster than expected, it was argued that it was now necessary to hedge against that potential by building the Safeguard ABM system.

The mad logic of the Peterkins ruled.

Sugar: They deploy the Tallinn, an anti-aircraft defense system.

Salt: On grounds that it can become an ABM system, we hedge and start to deploy Poseidons with their multiple warheads.

Sugar: They develop the SS-9 with its up to 20- to 25-megaton warhead capability.

Salt: We argue that they can deploy SS-9's faster than expected. The ABM is needed.

Sugar: Next, they will react against the "hard target" potential of our Poseidons, whether it exists or not. They must "assume" our small warheads have that capability.

That is the way the arms race escalates.

There are other examples, too. If we build the advanced manned strategic aircraft (AMSA), will not the Russians feel compelled to increase the number of their bombers, the defensive system needed to cope with AMSA, or their offensive weapons, or all three? And will this not, in turn, lead the military Establishment in this country to argue that, because the Russians have increased their proportionate effort, we must also increase the expenditure of our resources for additional weapons to meet their new threat?

And, because the escalation depends not on what they actually *do* and on what we actually *do,* but on the potential or capability of each, the sugar and the salt of new weapons are alternatively poured into the arms-race pot even before the genuine threat materializes. Ironically, much of this mutual escalation is based on speculation and conjecture.

The best thing for both the United States and Russia would be to take the advice of the Lady from Philadelphia. "Throw it all out." But, because neither country will act on that advice unilaterally, something else must be done. We must de-escalate terror. We must mutually reduce the potential for nuclear cataclysm. Even if we avoid destroying our world, unless we limit our mutual expenditures, we are both immeasurably harmed, economically, by what Secretary Mc-Namara has aptly described as the mad momentum of the arms race.

In the future, we can expect pressures for higher military budgets. This is true, despite public disenchantment over the excesses of military spending. Pressures will increase notwithstanding the loss of confidence in military judgments, which has stemmed from the Vietnam War and its daily casualty lists. The push for bigger military funds will come in spite of the counterpressures on the taxpayer's pocketbook from inflation, surcharges, and state and local taxes.

Even in the absence of increased threats from the Soviet Union or the Chinese Communists, the danger to the American economy is that military budgets will still continue to rise. They could rise not only absolutely but also proportionately. These pressures result from the changing nature of military weapons, the intelligence institutions created to assess military threats, the cumulative forces of inter-service rivalries, and the national and local economic pressures of those businesses and communities dependent on the military budget for their future.

What happened when Secretary Laird took over from Secretary Clifford demonstrates the way in which cumulative pressures for higher and higher defense budgets function. Each year, the Secretary of Defense delivers his posture statement. It provides the general setting and the rationale for the major program proposals in the military budget. The statement contains not only the immediate year's program, but outlines the setting in which military planning for the next five years will take place. On January 15, 1969, Secretary Clark Clifford forwarded a 165-page document to the Congress, explaining that:

> While neither law nor custom requires an outgoing Secretary
> of Defense to explain or justify the program or budget pro-

posals for the forthcoming fiscal year, the tradition of an "Annual Posture Statement" has been so firmly established by my predecessor, Robert S. McNamara, that I am reluctant to break it.

The single most important part of the document was the discussion of the strategic forces. Secretary Clifford restated the American policy of "deterrence" in these words:

> We must maintain at all times strategic forces of such size and character, and exhibit so unquestionable a will to use them in retaliation if needed, that no nation could ever conceivably deem it to its advantage to launch a deliberate nuclear attack on the United States or its allies.

Our policy is to remain so strong that no country could wipe us out, or rationally believe that it could wipe us out, in a "first strike." Our ability to retaliate deters others from launching a nuclear war. It is this policy of mutual terror that, we believe, has kept nuclear warheads in their silos since World War II.

The terms of strategic parlance must be understood. The ability to strike back as we have noted earlier, is called by the military planners our "assured destruction capability" and is defined as "the ability to inflict at all times and under all foreseeable conditions an unacceptable degree of damage upon any aggressor, or a combination of aggressors—even after absorbing a surprise attack."

In assessing our strategic nuclear policy, Secretary Clifford discussed the policy of deterrence based on our assured destruction capability under three separate conditions.

First, he discussed our actual, over-all strategic effectiveness as compared with the actual capabilities of the Soviet Union. This was a realistic assessment of the present capabilities of each.

Second, he discussed our assured destruction capability against the "Highest-Expected Threat" from the Soviet

Union as estimated in the National Intelligence Estimates.

Third, he discussed our capability for Assured Destruction in the 1970's against a "Greater-Than-Expected Threat" from the Soviet Union. This was an analysis of the adequacy of our forces in the "unlikely event that the Soviets move significantly beyond our highest expectations."

In considerable degree, Secretary Clifford's statement was reassuring. If that term seems to be a malapropism in the nuclear age, it was at least as reassuring as any statement could be.

First, he noted that, whereas the Soviet Union is moving vigorously to catch up with the United States in numbers of strategic missiles, it lagged well behind us in advanced missile technology. The Russians were deficient in missile accuracy, in MIRV development, and in penetration aids. After giving the actual numbers of land-based and sea-based missiles possessed by each country, and, after comparing the numbers of long- and short-range bombers each had in its strategic arsenal, Secretary Clifford gave this assessment of the quality of Soviet strategic weapons and defenses:

> Indeed, their new solid-fuel ICBM appears to be no better than our earliest Minuteman missiles, first deployed in FY 1963. Their new ballistic-missile submarine is probably most comparable to our earliest Polaris submarines, which first became operational about a decade ago. Their Galosh ABM system resembles in certain important respects the Nike-Zeus system, which we abandoned years ago because of its limited effectiveness. Their Bison and Bear long-range bombers are distinctly inferior to our B-52's, and we have long since eliminated from our forces the B-47's which were clearly superior to their Badger medium bombers.

There we have it. At the end of the 1960's, we were seven years ahead of the Russians in land-based ICBM's. We were a decade ahead of them in submarine missiles. Their ABM system, if it really was an ABM system, was one of a type we abandoned years ago. Their long-range bombers were vastly inferior. Their medium-range bombers were like ones we had already eliminated.

In terms of numbers, we had almost twice as many intercontinental missile launchers (1,710 to 945) and over four times as many intercontinental bombers (646 to 150) as the Soviet Union.

Those are the *facts*. Secretary Clifford's description of both the numbers and quality of the Soviet strategic forces was based on military realities and actual capability.

Secretary Clifford summed up his first point as follows:

> Accordingly, it is reasonable to conclude that even if the Soviets attempt to match us in numbers of strategic missiles we shall continue to have, as far into the future as we can now discern, a very substantial qualitative lead and a distinct superiority in the numbers of deliverable weapons and the over-all combat effectiveness of our strategic offensive forces.

"A very substantial qualitative lead" and a "distinct superiority in numbers" as "far into the future as we can now discern"—how much more do we need? But, suppose the National Intelligence Estimates contained mistakes of fact or errors of judgment? The military does not leave that to chance. Judging our real capability against a real threat, the Secretary examined two other possibilities.

The second calculation that is made in the National Intelligence Estimates is our assured destruction capability against the highest-expected threat. If the Russians were to strike us with every weapon we now know they have, and if these weapons were to function at their highest level of performance, what is our capability for assured destruction against the Soviet Union in case of that terrible event? Is our capability a genuine deterrent against such an event?

According to Secretary Clifford, even in these circumstances we had an awesome ability to hit back. In his words:

> Our calculations indicate that the U.S. strategic forces programmed over the next few years, even against the highest Soviet threat projected in the NIE, would be able to destroy in a second strike more than two-fifths of the Soviet population and about three-quarters of their industrial capacity.

If massive retaliation is a real deterrent, as our military planners obviously believe it is, we have such a deterrent. To use the informal parlance of a card game, we have it in spades. Even against the highest expected threat we could destroy two-fifths of the people and three-quarters of the industry in the Soviet Union with our retaliatory forces.

That would seem sufficient.

But Secretary Clifford was not content to end the calculations there. What would be our ability to hit back if there were "unexpected developments?" He outlined our capability to retaliate against a third contingency, namely in the case of a greater-than-expected threat from the Soviet Union.

The outgoing Secretary of Defense described a theoretical situation in which the Russians might take action to "degrade" the American assured destruction capability during the 1970's. Suppose the Russians were to develop and install highly accurate MIRV's in their large ICBM's? What would happen if they improved the accuracy of their missiles? What effect would it have on our assured destruction capability if they erected an effective ABM system? What would happen if they were to "deploy a large AWACS interceptor force with a good look-down, shoot-down capability, together with an extensive, effective low-altitude SAM system?"

The Secretary went on to say that:

> Any *one* of these actions would pose no particular threat to our "Assured Destruction Capability," but if they were to do all of these things simultaneously, which would appear to be

highly improbable on purely economic grounds, they might be able to degrade seriously the "assured Destruction Capability" of our strategic forces as presently planned.

On the basis that "all of these developments may occur, and occur simultaneously," Secretary Clifford reported a number of actions that had already been taken. It should be remembered that these actions were taken not to meet the actual threat the Soviet Union presented, nor even the highest expected threat, but to "place ourselves in a position where we can move forward promptly to meet any or all of the possible actions outlined under the 'Greater-Than-Expected Threat.' "

Minuteman III, Poseidon, and the missile-penetration-aids program would permit the country to cope with a large-scale Soviet ABM system—a Soviet ABM system that did not exist. To hedge against the possibility that the Russians might install MIRV's in their large ICBM's and greatly improve the accuracy of their smaller ICBM's, the Defense Department also initiated the development of a superhard silo for the Minuteman III, or a new, larger ICBM. Also, an early warning satellite was being developed and dispersal of bombers to secondary bases was undertaken to improve the survivability of our alert bombers from an SLBM attack.

To strengthen the penetration capabilities of our manned bombers against a possible, vastly improved Soviet air defense system, we were producing a new short-range attack missile (SRAM) and developing a new long range subsonic-cruise armed decoy (SCAD) for both our B-52 and FB-111 bombers.

In addition, Secretary Clifford reported that the Department was doing "preliminary development work on a new sea-based missile system (ULMS), a new land-based missile system and a new manned bomber."

Other steps also were possible to counter the greater-than-expected threat of the National Intelligence Estimates. They would offset the threat if the Russians were to do simultaneously all those things that Secretary Clifford said were "highly improbable" and that could degrade the assured destruction capability of our strategic forces, if carried out. Among these additional options, we could increase the proportion of bombers held on 15-minute ground alert from 40 to 60 per cent; expand the planned Sentinel system to include the defense of Minuteman sites; accelerate the deployment of Minuteman III; load the Poseidon with more warheads than presently planned; and construct new ballistic-missile submarines. Furthermore, the Secretary concluded, "If the emerging threat requires, we can accelerate deployment of a new, larger land-based or sea-based missile, a new manned bomber (AMSA), or all three."

He then warned, "We need not take any of these steps until we have some evidence that the threat is actually beginning to emerge," and he concluded that, "taking our strategic posture as a whole, we have an ample margin of safety and we can afford to proceed with due deliberation on very costly new programs."

The general public is unaware of the abundant strength this nation possesses. It is unaware that our budgets are based not on the sufficiency or the actual superiority in numbers and quality of our strategic system over the Soviet Union. The budget is based on meeting both the highest-expected and a very great proportion of the greater-than-expected threat of the Soviet Union.

It will be noted that, at the time of Clifford's statement, we had already, in many cases, taken action to cope with Soviet threats that, at the time, did not actually exist. We anticipated potential threats.

This is the problem of basing policy on such war-game terms as "assured destruction," "mutual deterrence," and "highest-expected" and "greater-than-expected" threats. Each side responds to a change in the other side's capability. Each side responds not only to an actual change in the other side's strategic capability, but to potential changes.

In *Agenda for the Nation* (Washington, D.C.: The Brookings Institution, 1968) Carl Kaysen stated:

> The present level of research, development, and production capacity for weapons on both sides is such that each has the power to respond to a change in the deployments of the other in a way that leaves it "satisfied" with its new position in relation to the adversary.

The unhappy results follow, namely:

> Each, accordingly, feels it must anticipate such a response. And so the arms race goes on. The expected result of the process can be no more than a new balance at higher force levels, larger expenditures, and most likely, unthinkable higher levels of destruction in the event that the forces were never used.

What we find ourselves in is a no-limit poker game with each side holding a royal flush. Its principal danger is that the odds against mankind's surviving the game are too high. Its secondary, but terribly deleterious effect is that, in the interval, not only the danger but the cost of the arms race escalates.

Given the present method of estimating strategic capabilities, the system contains a built-in, automatic, inevitable escalation device. As Kaysen has said, there is an "uncontrollable forward thrust of technical change in weaponry." Along with its high propensity to create terror, the system also creates virtually uncontrolled costs.

Not content with meeting the actual threat, the highest expected-threat, and major proportions of the greater-than-expected threat, Secretary Laird proposed, on March 19, 1969, two months after Secretary Clifford's posture statement was prepared, that the country take two additional steps among those options listed by Secretary Clifford, "if the emerging threat requires."

The original Sentinel ABM system was altered to defend the Minuteman missile sites. In his supplement to the 1970 posture statement, Laird also proposed that we accelerate development of a new manned bomber (AMSA).

Among the major reasons these steps were taken were the intelligence estimates that the Russians had gone forward with further deployment and further installation of the huge SS-9 missile.

Yet, actions taken previously as outlined by Secretary Clifford were for the purpose of offsetting "a Soviet ICBM force with a substantial hard-target kill capability."

To use the terrible jargon of modern warfare, we increased our offensive and defensive strategic forces in anticipation of a Soviet ICBM with a hard-target kill capability. Then, when they actually began to deploy and install the SS-9, we increased our offensive and defensive strategic forces again. We stepped up the development of the manned bomber AMSA. We deployed the Safeguard ABM.

Charles Schultze referred to this condition in his brilliant testimony before the 1969 Economy in Government Subcommittee hearings on "The Military Budget and National Economic Priorities." The former Director of the Bureau of the Budget testified:

I have seen several arguments as to why a new round in the strategic arms race will not be touched off by current U.S. policy.

I think they are dubious at best. One argument notes that the U.S. development of MIRV's and ABM is being made against a "greater-than-expected" threat—i.e., a Soviet threat larger than current intelligence estimates project. Hence, runs the argument, should the Soviets respond to our new developments, this response has already been taken into account in the "greater-than-expected" threat against which we are currently building.

Consequently, we would not have to respond ourselves with a still further strategic arms buildup, so the argument runs.

But this misses the very nature of "greater-than-expected" threat planning. Once the Soviets proceed to deploy a force which approaches the *current* "greater-than-expected" threat, then by definition a *new* "greater-than-expected" threat is generated, and additional strategic arms expenditures are undertaken to meet it.

"This is the heart of the dynamics of a strategic arms race," Schultze concluded. As George Santayana once remarked, fanaticism means redoubling one's efforts after having lost sight of one's aims. The mad momentum of the arms race explains why defense budgets are out of control. It is the reason behind the blank check for the military—the method, the system, and the dynamics by which the military gets its way.

But, in addition to the threats, highest-expected threats, and greater-than-expected threats, there are other reasons why the fiscal outlook is for higher and higher military budgets.

First and foremost is the pessimistic outlook for a large "fiscal dividend" when the Vietnam War ends. If the Pentagon has its way, the end of that war will bring no automatic release of all or even a very large part of the approximately $25 billion the Defense Department gave as the fiscal year 1970 cost of Vietnam.

The first and most detailed analysis of the lack of a substantial automatic Vietnam fiscal dividend was made by Charles Schultze. His estimates were later confirmed by Herbert Stein, of President Nixon's Council of Economic Advisers and a former fellow of the Brookings Institution. Others agree.

Secretary Laird stated shortly after he took office that

"even if we are successful in eliminating the war in Vietnam, our highest priority—we are still not going to come up with a drastically reduced defense budget—at least this Secretary of Defense will not recommend drastic reductions in defense spending, under presently foreseeable circumstances."

In his campaign for the Presidency, candidate Nixon stated only a few days before the election that he projected military budgets in 1972 at $85 billion or more, even with a reduction in the Vietnam War.

In testimony before our Subcommittee on Economy in Government, Robert C. Moot, the Comptroller of the Defense Department, testified that "a large reduction in the Defense budget should not be expected to follow automatically from cessation of hostilities in Vietnam."

Why will the end of the Vietnam War not result in billions of additional dollars either to increase our support of needed civilian priorities, to reduce taxes, or both?

Because he made both the first and the most penetrating analysis, let the points developed by former Budget Director Schultze answer that question. He makes a 5-year projection.

He estimates, first, in what I regard as a highly optimistic outlook, that the net growth in federal revenues during the first five years of the 1970's will be $70 billion.

To this, he adds a generous $20 billion in budgetary savings that would be available in eighteen months to two years after a ceasefire in Vietnam. The full $25 to $26 billion he attributed to Vietnam would not be saved since that figure includes a number of costs, such as the naval task forces and the B-52 bombers, which, if not in Vietnam, would be used on practice or training missions elsewhere. The $20 billion is, indeed, a most generous estimate. Comptroller Moot cites a figure of only $11 billion, calculated on a somewhat different basis, as the amount available in the short term after a Vietnam ceasefire.

From this total of $90 billion, Schultze calculates that "we must make several deductions before arriving at a net fiscal dividend freely available for domestic use." He cites the significant built-in growth in federal civilian expenditures. These include automatic increases in the interest on the national debt, veterans expenditures, Medicaid, increases associated with the growth in population, social security benefits, and others. He estimates that the "built-in" growth in civilian programs will cost some $35 billion. This leaves a dividend of $55 billion from which must be deducted an additional huge amount for non-Vietnam military spending, which he expects will rise significantly.

The almost inevitable increases in the non-Vietnam military costs take one's breath away. And these do not take into account the costs of mutual escalation of the strategic arms race.

The military spending excesses of the past will shortly become the problems of the future. There are numerous huge weapons systems in the offing. Some are planned. Others are authorized. Some have begun to be funded. Unless prompt action is taken, we may wake up and find that we are committed to billions upon billions of future expenditures. Costs will burgeon. Performance will continue to be substandard. Things may soon become a great deal worse than they have been.

Schultze named four key factors he sees as working toward an increase in the military budget.

First are the wage and salary increases for the 2.8 million men remaining in uniform and the civilian employees of the Pentagon, which will rise by about $1.5 billion per year or by $7.5 billion over the next five years.

Second are the future expenditure consequences of already approved weapon systems. Among those Schultze cited were:

1. The Minuteman III missile, with MIRV's; cost, $4.5 billion.
2. The Poseidon missile, with MIRV's; cost, including

the conversion of 31 Polaris submarines, $5.5 to $6.5 billion.

3. The Safeguard ABM system; minimum cost of $8 billion, plus hundreds of millions for annual operating costs.

4. The F-14 Navy fighter plane, which may replace the entire F-4 force of the Navy and Marine Corps; the 10-year investment and operational cost will exceed $20 billion.

5. A new F-15 air-to-air combat fighter for the Air Force.

6. Three nuclear attack carriers at a currently estimated cost of $525 to $540 million each.

7. Sixty-two new naval escort vessels, at an investment cost of nearly $5 billion.

8. A number of new amphibious assault ships.

9. A new Navy anti-submarine plane, the VSX, at a cost of $2 to $2.5 billion.

10. A new continental air defense system, including a complex "look-down" radar and an extensive modification program for the current F-106 interceptor.

In most cases, these systems have been approved, and procurement is under way. In some, such as the VSX, only the development is under way. Others are waiting in the wings, offstage, for future procurement.

Third, Schultze said that non-Vietnam defense expenditures will rise significantly, because of our old friend cost overruns, unless major steps are taken. The costs given above were current estimates. "But," as Schultze stated, when he gave his testimony, "past experience indicates that final costs of complex military hardware systems almost always exceed original estimates." Many have already gone up.

The C-5A, Minuteman II, and the Navy's submersible rescue vessel are familiar examples of ballooning expenditures. Schultze cited more. For example, a study of missile systems in the 1950's and early 1960's revealed that the average unit cost of missiles was 3.2 times the original estimates.

The nuclear carrier *Nimitz*, now under construction, was estimated in 1967 to cost $440 million. One year later, the estimate was raised to $536 million. No new estimates have been released, but, given the rapidly rising cost of shipbuilding, it is almost certain that this latter figure will be exceeded. In January, 1968, the Defense Department proposed a plan for building 68 naval escort vessels at a total cost of $3 billion. In January, 1969, the estimated costs of that program had risen to $5 billion. The cost of modernizing the carrier *Midway* was originally given as $88 million, and the work was scheduled to be completed in 24 months. In January, 1969, the cost estimate was doubled, to $178 million, and the time estimate also doubled, to 48 months.

The Air Force's manned orbiting laboratory (the MOL) was originally announced by President Johnson at a cost of $1.5 billion. It was later estimated at $3 billion. In the case of the MOL, the program was stopped in the summer of 1969 when pressures from Congress forced a cut in defense expenditures, but already the $1.5 billion had been spent.

Fourth, and finally, Schultze listed a series of weapons systems that were under development and were advocated strongly by the Joint Chiefs of Staff, but that had not yet been approved for deployment. Among his items were the AMSA, on which the investment cost will no doubt be a minimum of $10 billion, and the new main battle tank, now in production engineering. Depending on the number of tanks purchased, a procurement decision will involve investment costs of $1 to $1.5 billion. In addition, a new attack aircraft, the AX, is under development for the Air Force; the Navy is proposing a major shipbuilding and reconversion program to replace or modernize large numbers of its older vessels; a new continental air defense interceptor, the F-12, is being advocated by the Air Force; and a new underwater strategic missile system (the ULMS) is under development for the Navy.

As Schultze told our Subcommittee, after detailing these weapons systems under development, "In the normal course of events, not all of these new systems will be adopted in the next five years. But, in the normal course of events, some will be."

He calculated that his first three items alone—the increase in civilian and military pay, the annual costs of the approved weapon systems, and allowing for only modest cost escalation by individual systems—would increase non-Vietnam military expenditures by almost $20 billion over the fiscal year 1969 figure.

According to his testimony, this modest sum "leaves *out* of account the possibility of more than modest cost escalation, the adoption of large new systems like the AMSA, and a further round of strategic arms escalation."

The net 5-year fiscal dividend from the Vietnam War, based on Schultze's assumptions, comes to $35 billion or $7 billion a year. Much, if not all of this, could be eaten up in new weapons systems, a few big overruns, or a Middle East crisis.

This pessimistic view of the fiscal dividend is shared by Comptroller of the Defense Department Moot, who speaks also of "meeting the backlogs which have accumulated" because of the emphasis on Vietnam. He talks of construction projects foregone, needed equipment maintenance, and modernization of the forces not deployed in Southeast Asia. He mentions the need to reconstitute inventory levels as production phases down. When these are added to Schultze's calculations, the former Director of the Budget Bureau's projections may prove very optimistic.

With respect to post-Vietnam expenditures, the Defense Department is attempting to pre-empt the field. Their plans are ready. Their programs are drawn up. In some cases, the weapons are funded. Others are already deployed. The military services are ready with their plans and their programs to grab most, if not all, of the $26 billion to $30 billion spent on the fighting. Their efforts are re-enforced by the annual posture statement. They are ready with new weapons and systems. They have contructed a rationale to support their interests. The issue is one of priorities. The question is how to cut the national economic pie, at the end of the war.

Unless there is a conscious, determined effort to rearrange priorities, the billions being spent, at this writing, on the Vietnam War will be eaten up by built-in increases and new Pentagon spending on old and new weapons systems of ever madder megatonnage.

X

Bringing the Military Budget
Under Control

WHAT WE FACE in the United States in the 1970's is a massive
clash between the military and civilian needs, within both
the military and civilian sectors. This conflict is taking place
on several levels at the same time.

At one level is the fight over waste, inefficiency, and mismanagement within the Defense Department. This is a non-
ideological fight, which attracts hawks and doves alike. Many
of those anxious to provide their country with all the weapons and security it needs are, nonetheless, appalled at the
wasteful procedures and inefficient management of the Pentagon. The time has arrived when many of the strongest advocates of strength and preparedness are unwilling to vote
funds, or authorize new weapons systems, or accept the military justifications for them, except after the most critical
review.

218

At another level is the conflict over priorities. It examines the alternatives to spending the money for weapons system A as against weapons system B. It also questions funds for a weapons system, on the one hand, as against a high-level civilian priority, on the other.

The question of what might have been purchased for the $2 billion overrun on the C-5A illustrates the point.

Two billion dollars is a phenomenal amount of money, although it is the amount by which costs exceeded estimates on one weapon system alone. The alternatives to spending that amount of money on one overrun are almost limitless.

The $2 billion at $10,000 per man per year would finance the pay and allowances and associated personnel costs for 200,000 combat troops, or more than ten combat divisions for a full year. That is why many of us say the country could be stronger, if we spent defense funds more efficiently. There are priorities within the military budget as well as between it and the civilian needs.

Two billion dollars would pay for the housing subsidy under the new homeowners' section of the 1968 Housing Act for some three and one-third million families for an entire year. Yet the full $100 million requested for that program for the entire country has not been funded, although it is only one-twentieth the C-5A overrun.

The $2 billion overrun on one airplane contract would finance all the economic assistance or Agency for International Development (AID) funds in the original 1970 budget of $1.973 billion.

The $2 billion is five times the amount in the budget for rural electrification. It is more than five times the amount the Interior Department will spend on all forms of recreation.

The $2 billion estimated overrun on the C-5A is almost twenty times the $212 million in the Department of Transportation budget for urban mass transit and the high-speed ground transportation programs, which are desperately needed. It is almost double the amount of all the funds in the

1970 Department of Housing and Urban Development budget for all low and moderate-income housing, which is even more desperately needed than good transportation.

The $2 billion would pay for almost all non-service-connected pensions for all U.S. veterans for fiscal year 1970. It is more, by $300 million, than all the money we spend on veterans' hospitals and medical care.

It is almost three times the $742 million in the budget for law enforcement, the administration of justice, and civil rights. This comparison forcefully raises the question of what kind of priority system we have when $2 billion can be wasted, while our courts are jammed, the crime rate has risen, and millions of Americans still suffer the stigma and indignities of second-class citizenship?

At the two levels of wastefulness and of priorities, great reforms could be made. There is also a third level at which the battle for critical review is brewing. This is over questions of our commitments and our responsibilities in the world. The answers to these questions could drastically affect both our defense budget and the kind of world in which we live.

But it is entirely possible for us to keep our present commitments and reduce both the actual and relative defense budget. It is also possible to reduce our commitments and yet, through waste and profligate spending, increase defense expenditures.

The immediate danger we face is an escalation in both spending and terror. The dynamics of one feed on the dynamics of the other. The time has arrived when, for the sake of our country and the world, we must reduce them both.

But how? How can we reduce military expenditures, cut the power of the military-industrial complex, and rearrange our priorities? How can we keep the country strong and free without the military procurement excesses of the past?

Effective arms control and an end to the international arms race are the fundamental ways to cut expenditures and assure our security.

But we need not wait for that to happen before coming to grips with the excesses of the military budget. Well short of the happy day when that comes to pass, other things can be done. They can be done without affecting our real military strength and security. They can save billions without cutting military muscle. We must foster, in the executive branch of the government, the same climate of criticism and concern that, this past season, seized almost half the Senate when it examined the ABM decision. In fact, this climate is much more important than either procedural changes or institutional arrangements. Only when the whole government feels that it is free to question defense expenditures can changes be made. As Charles Schultze stated, in his testimony before the Subcommittee on Economy in Government, concerning the way the Budget Bureau examined the military funds in the past:

> The Budget Bureau can effectively dig into and review what the President wants it to review under this procedure or many others. It can raise questions of budgetary priorities—questioning, for example the worth of building forces against a particular set of contingencies on grounds of higher priority domestic needs—when and only when the President feels that *he* can effectively question military judgments on those grounds.

In the Cold War environment, when criticism made one vulnerable to the charge of playing fast and loose with the national security, neither the President nor Congress could question military judgments. Even now, to question military omniscience is to lay oneself open to allegations of being a "new isolationist." That was the label used for critics by President Nixon in a speech at the Air Force Academy. Nonetheless, there is a new climate of criticism in Congress.

Far from calling for anything like a return to the isolationism of the 1930's, today's congressional critics seek an efficient defense system that will keep our country strong and free, without threatening our economic capacity or our traditional freedoms.

This new climate of criticism must be nurtured if fundamental positions are to be questioned. The first pressing need is to review the strategic concept on which our defense posture is based—the two-and-one-half war policy. Should it be the policy of the United States to prepare itself to fight a major land war in Europe, a major land war in Asia, and a minor war, say in the Caribbean, all at the same time? This policy must be re-examined.

Second, are we now providing a disproportionate share of the troops, the ships, the funds, and the support for the defense of Europe? If the Europeans feel so secure that they are unwilling to fulfill their military commitments for their own safety, are we obligated to fulfill them? If they do not fear for their security, should we?

Third, the strategic and tactical concepts by which we maintain 429 major bases and 2,972 minor bases on every continent throughout the world should be re-examined. Do we need that many bases? Do we need them where they are? Do we need them for the purposes for which they were originally established?

These fundamental policies upon which the present defense forces of the United States are based should receive the most searching review. The commitments we have to some forty nations of the world should be reconsidered.

But even within the framework of the present strategic concepts, numerous changes can be made that could vastly reduce the amount of our military expenditures without cutting our military strength. Essentially, these changes are of two types.

The first are procedural or institutional changes that would give us the knowledge and develop the machinery to carry out more effective policies.

The second are the proposals for specific savings. They detail the specific programs, weapons, and practices that can be cut or changed without weakening the defense of the country. In this area, we should not only be concerned with the efficiencies of procurement but also with the issue of what is to be procured.

Let us first examine the proposed procedural and institutional changes needed to make for more efficient and effective military policies.

Foreign policy should be returned to the province of the President and the State Department. To carry this out, I have already proposed that an annual posture statement should be presented to Congress by the Secretary of State in order to emphasize the role of foreign policy in our basic decisions and de-emphasize the role now played by the Pentagon in presenting the only "posture" statement we receive. It is here that the two-and-one-half war policy should be discussed, here that our relationships to NATO and Western Europe should be examined, here that our overseas military bases and their effects on foreign policy should be reviewed.

In the field of military contracting, a similar shift from military to civilian control should take place. Procurement of military hardware and contracts for military research and development should be carried out by an independent civilian agency.

At the present time, each service is judge and jury over its own contracting. Because of their overwhelming self-interest in the procurement of particular weapons, the individual services are unable to judge contracting critically. Moreover, within the services, the few independent civilian cost experts they now have depend on their military superiors for pro-

motion. The good ones, like the A. E. Fitzgeralds, are fired
or sent to some armed forces Siberia. There is now no meaningful supervision over contract costs.

Immediate objections to the proposal of establishing a su-
pervisory civilian agency can be expected. The military out-
cries may exceed the decibel levels of the jet planes from
Washington's National Airport, which take off adjacent to
the Pentagon's Mall entrance.

But the proposal would retain in the hands of the Joint
Chiefs and the military the decisions as to what weapons are
needed and what specifications they should meet. The requirements should then be turned over to a completely independent agency, such as the Department of Commerce, the
General Services Administration, or a special agency under
civilian control established for this single purpose of handling all military procurement and contracting. Britain's
Ministry of Technology, which now performs precisely such
a function and performs it very well indeed, could serve as a
model. The agency should make cost-effective analyses
studies, provide "should-cost" studies, do the actual contracting, and supervise the manufacturers' performances.

Issues such as the need to change specifications due to a
shift in military requirements during the term of the contract
could still be determined by the military services. But the
contracting should be carried out independently of the Air
Force, Navy, Army, or Marine Corps. The principle should
be to let the military fight and determine the weapons it
needs to fight if it can convince the President, Congress, and
the American people they are needed. Let the civilians pro-
cure the weapons under rigid, businesslike procedures.

In view of the excessive costs of past military weapons, excessive delays in delivery, the wholesale reduction of specifications during their manufacture, and the fantastic failures
in performance, there is no valid argument against such an
independent procurement and contracting agency. It could

not possibly do worse than has been done under existing procedures. It could save billions, while strengthening our military posture.

In addition to these major institutional changes, a series of others should be made.

The Budget Bureau must make certain that the reorganization of its manpower and its procedures provides a really effective review of the military budget. It must improve upon the practice of assigning only 10 per cent of its personnel to examine the 80 per cent of the controllable budget that the military requests represent. It must subject the military budget requests to the same hard examination it gives to poverty programs, housing for the poor, and requests for health, welfare, and education.

There has been one fundamental failure by the President, by the Bureau of the Budget, by the Pentagon itself, by the congressional Armed Services and Appropriation committees, and by the General Accounting Office, with respect to their review of Pentagon requirements. That has been the failure to change the review procedures to reflect the fundamental shift in the nature of weapons and their procurement. The shift from trucks, tanks, planes, and guns to highly sophisticated missiles and the radar and computers and gyroscopes that make them function has been accompanied by enormous complications in technology. The executive and legislative institutions have failed to change their procedures to reflect the shift from the old military contractors, who produced military weapons as a modest part of their business, to the new aerospace industry, which is almost exclusively dependent on the military for its survival.

At every level of review there has been a fantastic failure. At the present time, no one at any level or within any branch of the government adequately performs a watchdog function over military spending. This is the result, in part, of the generally uncritical atmosphere of the 1950's and the 1960's. It is also due to the failure to shift emphasis away from the review of the traditional military budget items to a critical examination of the sophisticated modern weapons system and their acquisition process. Through the establishment in the Pentagon of the Defense Supply Agency, the procurement of shoes, shirts, underwear, and belts has been brought under control. But the purchases of black boxes, avionics, missiles, and weapons remains uncontrolled.

A reorganization of institutions at every level—the White House, the Budget Bureau, the Pentagon, the Congress, and the General Accounting Office—must be made in order that we may judge, analyze, criticize, review, and recommend policies to control the procurement of modern weapons systems.

These institutions must set up the procedures and hire the personnel to make a separate, highly competent, highly skeptical, and penetrating review of the Department of Defense budget in a way in which it has never been done before. Very well-trained analysts using all the modern tools are needed to examine critically the large proportion of the controllable budget that military requests represent.

In addition, a system of "zero-based" budgeting should be instituted by the individual services, at the Department of Defense, and at the Budget Bureau itself. The reviews of budget items should be made each year from the ground up. We should no longer accept uncritically last year's budget for any item. Merely examining with some slight critical sense the added increment for the new year is wholly inadequate. We should move to "zero-based" budgeting at all levels.

To achieve these contracting and procurement reforms, two additional ingredients are needed. First, a system of severe penalties should be instituted against contractors who fail in any important contractual requirement.

The "buy-in bidding" practice could be stopped if the contractor were required to bear the difference between his bid and the real cost.

Penalties should be assessed for late delivery.

Contractors who fail to meet specifications, or change them deliberately, should be made ineligible for future contracts.

In many cases of excessively costly weapons systems, Congress would not have gone ahead on them if the true costs had been known. In the future, Congress must get responsible and accurate estimates. And, in turn, Congress and the President must provide a system of penalties for those contractors and military and civilian procurement officers who make wrong estimates. A few canceled contracts would be a powerful antidote to waste. Similarly, military and civilian officials who fail in their duties should be denied future promotions and advancement in position.

We also need a real change in the attitude of the military services toward contracting. In the past, we have been told too often that matters were under constant review, that the service was always "striving to do better," and was "dedicated to cutting waste." We have heard cliché after cliché.

What we have missed from both Pentagon and Administration officials is any sense of urgency. We have seen no determination to get the job done. We need someone to lay down the law, pound the table, crack heads together, cancel a few contracts, fire some procurement officials, deny promotion to military program managers, and cut an agency's budget. Then we will get change and action.

In addition, immediate steps must be taken to reverse the increase in the percentage of non-negotiated contracts and to increase the amount of truly competitive bid contracts.

Although major improvements have been made in the number of items bought and stored under the unified Defense Supply Agency, we must attack the problem of excesses and surpluses. Surpluses of as much as 28 per cent of the total amount of supplies is an altogether unwarranted figure. Such excesses must be brought to an end.

The Truth in Negotiations Act, which was enacted in September, 1962, should be strengthened. It requires that contracting officers obtain current, accurate, and complete cost data in the process leading to the award of negotiated contracts. It has virtually served as the taxpayer's only defense against overpricing on negotiated contracts. Yet it has never been adequately enforced and it does not have enough teeth. Legislation is needed to make the *submission* of cost and pricing data mandatory under the Act for all contracts awarded other than through formally advertised price competition procedures.

We also need legislation to establish uniform guidelines for all federal agencies on the use of patents obtained for inventions made under U.S. Government contracts.

The conflict-of-interest statutes should be amended to prevent military officers and civilian officials, for a period of at least two years after leaving the Pentagon, from going to work for a contractor with whom they have had direct dealings in their work at the Pentagon.

In addition to all these measures, before a number of reforms can happen, the President, Congress, and the Defense Department need far more good information than is presently provided. Numerous suggestions were made by the witnesses who appeared before the Subcommittee on Economy in Government, and in the Joint Economic Committee's Interim Report.

Members of the Committee proposed that the General Accounting Office should conduct a comprehensive study of profitability in defense contracting. We proposed that the study should include historical trends of "going in" and actual profits considered both as a percentage of costs and, most importantly, as a return on investment. The only existing profitability study we have is one done by the Institute of Logistics Management, a Defense Department–dependent group, whose figures are without significant merit.

My amendment to the 1969 military authorization bill gave the General Accounting Office much of the additional authority it said it needed to carry out a comprehensive profitability study of major defense contractors. The amendment remained in the bill when signed into law, but changes by the Conference Committee now leave the issue of whether we get a first-rate study of profits up to the GAO and, in cases where contractors refuse to provide the necessary information, to the Armed Services Committee.

The Joint Economic Committee also proposed in its May, 1969, Report that the GAO should develop a "weapons acquisition status" report. In short, it called for an "overrun" report to be made on a timely basis.

The hearings we held on the C-5A and the facts, which we brought out, on the $2 billion overrun were the first ever developed on an overrun on a major weapons system while there was still time to act. Less than five planes of the 120 proposed had been completed when our facts were developed. The second batch of 62 planes, or Run B, had not been ordered when we revealed the tremendous overrun. We pointed out that the act of ordering Run B would trigger the "escalation clause" and the "repricing formula" in the contract. For the first time, facts were available about an overrun that made it possible for the military to cut its losses drastically. But instead of heeding advice, the Air Force, in January, 1969, ordered Run B, triggered the escalation clause and repricing formula, and ensured a multibillion-dollar overrun. But, the facts were available on a timely basis. The blame is clear. It was this brazen act on the part of the Air Force that leads me to propose that military contracting be carried out by an independent civilian agency.

The substance of my proposal for a "quarterly overrun"

report on major weapons systems was carried out in the Schweiker amendment to the military authorization bill. The amendment was killed, unfortunately, in the Conference Committee. But the GAO is providing such reports.

Another body of information sorely needed is that on the exchange of personnel between the Defense Department and defense industry. This principle was carried out in my amendment to the military authorization bill calling for annual disclosure by the Secretary of Defense of both civilian and military officials who moved from the corridors of the Pentagon to the plants of the contractors, as well as those who moved from industry board rooms into Pentagon offices. The disclosure amendment did not ask for information of a personal nature. On the one hand, it called for disclosure of what contracts or weapons systems the officer or official had been involved with at the Pentagon. On the other hand, it asked what contracts or what weapons systems his new employer held.

Other types of information are badly needed, too. We need to know the amount of "progress payments" made to contractors compared with the actual work segments they have completed. In the past, these have been paid out on the basis of "costs incurred" rather than "work completed," which has amounted to little more than the provision of interest-free working capital to them.

Congress should know how the actual performance standards of weapons compare with their original specifications and requirements. Are we getting a dollar's worth of performance for every dollar spent?

Information on the number and effect of contract changes should be available to those in the executive branch and Congress who review military contracting.

The Defense Department should collect complete data on subcontracting, including the total amount of subcontracts awarded, the number of competitive and negotiated awards, subcontract profits, type of work subcontracted out, the relationship between the prime contractor and the subcontractor, and compliance with the Truth in Negotiations Act. The present void in subcontracting information should be filled.

This is the kind of specific information needed to reform the entire system of contracting now in force at the Pentagon. One prerequisite for getting that information is the institution of a uniform system of accounting among military contractors as Admiral Rickover has repeatedly called for. It is especially important that the uniform system provide a method to measure profit on the actual investment of the companies rather than on their costs or sales.

Still other information is needed by both Congress and the country if some of the broader defects and abuses in military spending are to be corrected.

Former Budget Director Charles Schultze proposed that the defense posture statement should incorporate a five-year projection of the future expenditure consequences of current and proposed military force levels, weapons procurement, etc.

I call this the "know-what-you're-getting-into" recommendation.

As Schultze testified, "This need not, and should not, be an attempt to forecast *future* decisions. But, he said, it should, in effect, contain "the five-year budgetary consequences of past decisions and of those proposed in the current budget request."

One of the basic problems with defense expenditures is the "foot-in-the-door" technique described at the beginning of this book. The first-year expenditure is often very small. According to Schultze:

> Hence it is quite possible in any one year for the Congress to authorize and appropriate, in sum, a relatively small amount for several new systems which, two to five years in the future. use up a very large amount of budgetary resources.

In addition to a 5-year projection of costs, he recommended that the posture statement include cost data on specific elements and components of the military forces and weapons. For example, what is the annual cost of the forces we maintain against the possibility of a Chinese attack in Southeast Asia? In other words, how much do we spend against that one-war possibility of the two-and-one-half war policy?

How much does it cost to construct and operate a naval attack-carrier force? It is not the cost of the carrier alone. Also included must be the Navy air wings on board and in reserve; the cruisers, destroyers, and submarines that protect the carrier; lost time in port; and the huge training and other costs associated with it. Present estimates are in the neighborhood of $2 billion a year. With that kind of information seriously examined would we be as willing as we have been in the past to authorize an additional carrier for the limited mission it can perform?

As Schultze put it, "These are precisely the kinds of information needed to make possible a rational and responsible debate about the military budget in the context of national priorities."

Additional general economic information is needed, too, if we are to measure accurately the effect of military spending on the economy and to judge between and among priorities.

We need a military procurement cost index to show the prices of military end products paid by the Department of Defense, and the cost of labor, materials, and capital used to produce the military end products. As a result of the Report of the Economy in Government Subcommittee on the Economics of Military Procurement, the General Accounting Office, and the Departments of Defense, Commerce, and Labor have met with the Committee staff to work out means of developing such a cost index.

In the general area of the economic effects of military procurement, the Council of Economic Advisers must play a much bigger role than it has in the past. Presently, less than two pages of the President's annual Economic Report is devoted to an analysis of defense spending. That fact alone speaks volumes when it is remembered that such spending is the largest single item in the federal government's budget, when it is responsible for increased taxes, spiraling costs, pressure on labor markets, shortages of materials, and the uneconomic use of resources. In this and almost all other areas of military procurement, no one has been tending the store.

Yet, this information is vitally needed if the President and Congress are to do an effective job of overseeing the military budget.

Let us turn to the question of specifics, as opposed to procedural and institutional changes. Where can the military budget be cut? How can we cut up to $10 billion without affecting our combat strength? How can we do this either under existing arrangements or in the framework of proposals such as both Schultze and I have made about a foreign policy posture statement and the reorganization of Congress to receive and analyze information?

The first candidate for attention is manpower. About half the total defense budget goes for manpower and associated costs. A number of steps should be taken.

The ratio of supply and support troops to actual combat troops is excessively high in the American military services. While the Russians have a ratio of roughly three to one, we have a ratio of about ten to one. (In Vietnam, the ratio of combat infantry riflemen to all other troops was estimated at one to forty.) A reduction in our ratio to nine to one could reduce our forces by 350,000. At $10,000 per man per year, that could bring $3.5 billion a year in savings without cutting combat efficiency. In fact, we would no doubt be stronger and more efficient.

Robert S. Benson, the former "Whiz Kid" quoted else-where in these pages, urges additional manpower cuts. He believes that $50 million a year could be saved if the Army followed the same basic training policy as the Navy and Air Force now follow. Except for men destined for combat duty, the latter two services have a reduced period of basic training and speed men into the specialized training for the actual work they will perform during their period in the service. Some $500 million a year could be saved by reducing changes in military assignments by one-fourth. In this age of specialization, it is clearly ridiculous for servicemen to change assignments about once a year. This half-billion in savings would come from the reduction in transportation and moving costs alone. More could be saved in terms of a serviceman's improved efficiency on a job he stayed with.

Benson also argues that an additional $450 million could be saved by reforming the Pentagon's method of calculating leave policy and manpower requirements. Instead of requiring units to absorb absences due to leave, illness, training, and transfer, the Pentagon increases requirements for these needs. Private business includes them in its ordinary requirements. In addition, the thirty-days-a-year leave policy for all forces is far in excess of either private business or general government practice. Except for those on hardship or combat duty, men who work a routine 5-day, 40-hour, no-overtime week should receive leave time on a basis comparable with their civilian government opposite numbers.

The detailed study in July, 1968, of military requirements by the *Congressional Quarterly*, noted earlier, confirmed that huge savings in manpower could be made. Relying entirely on Pentagon sources not unfriendly to military requirements, *CQ* estimated that $4.2 billion could be saved by cutting manpower 10 per cent and requiring each service to absorb the manpower requirements of troops in transit between assignments. This confirms Benson's estimates.

Conservatively, about $4 billion could be saved from the almost $80 billion annual defense budget by a more efficient use of manpower.

A second major area where sharp cuts could be made is in reducing or cutting out nonessential programs. Among the candidates are the public relations activities of the Pentagon and the individual services on which we could not only save money but, by so doing, promote a much healthier atmosphere, since much of the alleged public relations is a disguised form of propaganda. In addition, the numerous free flights and inspection trips to Air Force bases provided for local business and community leaders should be abolished. The fleet of military planes available for high-ranking officers also should be cut. Commercial flights would, in most cases, be cheaper.

The funds spent for research that is not mission-oriented, to schools and colleges for social science and behavioral studies, for foreign policy studies, to universities and businesses overseas, and for indefinite and nondefined general research unassociated with any weapon or definite military need, should all be drastically cut or stopped altogether. Well over $1 billion is involved. And surely, the Department of Defense is not the appropriate agency to conduct foreign area and foreign policy research projects—especially not the one to monopolize the field, as it does, with an annual budget of $6.2 million for policy research, overshadowing the State Department's $4.1 million for its Bureau of Intelligence and Research, and with $7.5 million for area research, compared to the State Department's meager $125,000. It is not the appropriate agency to wage what the Pentagon's chief researcher, Dr. John Foster, has termed "peacefare." In the research in social science and human behavior it conducts through its sixteen captive think tanks, the Senate Foreign Relations Committee "found evidence of much duplication and waste of taxpayers' money" in that small part of the $300 million a year of such activities the Committee looked at in 1969.

The abuses associated with the PX's and commissaries should be reviewed and cut. The original purposes of both, namely, to provide services in remote areas or to prevent local merchants from gouging troops, have long since become irrelevant. They now absorb too much time and personnel, provide services to retired and some ineligible civilians for groceries, gasoline, auto repairs, consumer durables, and other items that were never remotely intended to be given.

The Defense Department should get out of much non-defense business. It still owns and operates shipyards. Over $15 billion in industrial plant and machinery is government-owned. The practice of interest-free progress payments to contractors should end.

A great many gimmicks that use manpower and create vast paperwork should be done away with. The services should reduce or stop, because of their obvious ineffectiveness, such programs as PERT, PEP, Value Engineering, Human Engineering, and the Zero Defects concept. The mere list of names makes one shudder. We should resist new gimmicks, such as Total Package Procurement and the Milestone Buying System. All of these essentially substitute form for substance. A saving of $500 million should be possible from cutting these nonessential items alone.

A review of the 429 major and 2,972 minor bases the military owns or leases in thirty countries throughout the world should bring at least a $1 billion saving in the $4.5 billion we now spend on them annually. A reduction in our $2.5 billion annual balance-of-payments drain would result as well.

I agree with Admiral Rickover that a $2 billion saving could come from instituting a uniform accounting system alone. A total of more than $7 billion could thus surely be cut from manpower, nonessential public relations and other contracts and services, closing nonessential overseas bases, and instituting a uniform accounting system.

A final $2.5 billion in savings could surely be made in contracting and weapons systems procurement. With the institutional changes needed at the Budget Bureau, by the Council of Economic Advisers, in the Pentagon, at the General Accounting Office, and in the way Congress examines the military budget, intelligent challenges to weapons-systems policies can be made. More prototypes can be built before rushing into volume production. This could save billions on weapons systems and modern avionics. Genuine cost effectiveness analyses by the Bureau of the Budget, the Pentagon, and Congress should bring major challenges to newly proposed and inefficient weapons.

The unduly sophisticated electronic systems for tactical aircraft should be modified at a saving of hundreds of millions. The eight ASW (anti-submarine warfare) carriers, never effective in locating or destroying a modern submarine, should be abandoned. Attack submarines, land-based patrol planes, destroyers, and other means should be substituted. The potential savings run as high as $400 million. The AMSA should not be built unless a far stronger case is presented. A minimum of $2 billion can be saved by not building the prototypes. Refusing to move into production will save a minimum of $10 billion to $12 billion.

Building additional nuclear-powered attack carriers in the missile age appears outdated. The $2 billion a year for each new attack carrier and its supporting vessels at stake is not a net saving, as some additional costs would have to be met for functions the carriers could perform less well. Nonetheless, huge funds are involved. Other weapons such as the Fast Deployment Logistic Ships (FDL's), the entire chemical and biological warfare (CBW) issue, the Main Battle Tank (MBT-70), the F-14 fighter plane, additional submersible Submarine Rescue Vessels, and the size and number of our amphibious forces, should all be placed under intensive review to determine if the added functions they provide are worth the huge additional costs.

These are the institutional, procedural, and substantive changes needed to bring military spending under control. If we can effect them, the day of the blank check for the military will finally end. But not until then will we begin to find our way out of the military-industrial wasteland into which we have wandered.

For the sake of the security of the country and the welfare of the American people, the time has come to call a halt to the extravagances and excesses of the military-industrial complex. There is no reason why, if we control our military expenditures, bring our world commitments into line, and establish sensible priorities for government spending, we cannot keep our nation truly strong and free.

Appendix

TABLE 1.—C-5A PROGRAM GROWTH
[In millions of dollars]

	Original estimate [1]	October 1968 estimate [2]	Difference
R. & D. (5 aircraft):			
Lockheed	514.1	607.0	92.9
GE	242.7	285.9	43.2
Add	220.2	109.8	[3](−110.4)
Total	977.0	1,002.7	25.7
Run A (53 aircraft):			
Lockheed	892.4	1,157.4	265.0
GE	216.0	[4] 236.7	20.7
Add	101.6	157.0	55.4
Total	[5] 1,210.0	1,551.1	341.1
Total R. & D. + run A	2,187.0	2,553.8	366.8
Run B (62 aircraft):			
Lockheed	538.8	. . . .	. . . .
Add (5) [6]	61.0	. . . .	. . . .
Total Lockheed	599.8	1,404.3	804.5
GE	172.9	. . . .	. . . .
Add (5) [6]	12.5	. . . .	. . . .
Total GE	185.4	[4] 230.3	44.9
Total add	105.8	173.7	67.9
Total Run B	891.0	1,808.3	917.3
AFLC investment	293.0	968.0	675.0
Total program	3,371.0	5,330.1	1,959.1

Source: The *Congressional Record*, September 4, 1969.

TABLE 2.—UNIT COSTS
DERIVED FROM PROGRAM ESTIMATE

	Original estimate	October 1968 estimate	Original unit cost	October 1968 unit cost
R. & D. (5)	977	1,002.7	. . . .	. . .
Run A (53)	1,210	1,551.1	22.8	29.3
Run B (62)	891	1,808.3	14.4	29.2
Spares (AFLC)	293	968.0	. . . .	. . .
Total, including (120) R. & D.	3,371	5,330.1	28.1	43.4

1 Total figures based upon April 1965 independent cost estimate except as shown in footnote 5. Contractor amounts are contract values as of October 1965. Add is the residual between ICE and contract values.

2 Total figures are obtained from October 1968 C-5A cost trace summary. Estimated contractor prices to be paid by the Government ASD cost team estimate of October 1968 which indicates anticipated Air Force price at that time, except as noted in footnote 4. Add figures are a residual between cost trace and contractor prices.

3 Since the add figures are a residual between program cost estimates and estimated contractor cost to the Government they can be expected to decrease as the program progresses.

4 Figures for GE current estimated price to the Government has been made to reconcile to $467,000,000 as shown on the C-5A program cost estimate October 1968 funding requirements versus August 1968 PCR for production run A, run B, and 5 run C. This amount is $76,400,000 under what is shown as the price to the Government at that time. As near as can be determined, the difference is the result of not including the 69 spare engines which were one of the production options (i.e., 69/564 × $631,000,000) as shown on pp. 1–5 of the Whittaker report.

5 Run A totals have been reduced from the independent cost estimate figure by $23,000,000—the average cost of 1 aircraft and 1 set of engines since the ICE run A was for 54 aircraft rather than the present 53 aircraft.

6 $61,000,000 and $12,500,000 have been added to the contract amounts to add in the last 5 aircraft which brings the total up to 120 craft. They were shown as run C at the time of the independent cost estimate.

Source: The *Congressional Record*, September 4, 1969.

Index

Acheson, Secretary of State Dean, 41, 191
Adams, Maj. Gen. R. H., 159
Advanced manned strategic aircraft (AMSA), 68, 69, 70, 71, 72, 73, 74, 115, 126, 155, 201, 208, 210, 216
Aerospace Manufacturer's Council, 142
Agency for International Development (AID), 219
Agenda for the Nation (Kaysen), 209
Air Force Academy, 222
Air Force Guidebook, 49
Air Force Plant No. 6, 50
Alness, Lt. Gen. H. T., 157, 165
American Federation of Labor–Congress of Industrial Organizations (AFL-CIO), 21, 146
American Ordnance Association, 148
American Political Science Association's Distinguished Service Award, 107
American Smelting and Mining Company, 143

American Telephone and Telegraph Company, 14, 16, 19, 135
Americans for Constitutional Action, 148
Amphibious assault ships, 214
Anti-ballistic missile (ABM), 9, 16, 20, 21, 22, 23, 64, 65, 70, 72, 73, 92, 93, 98, 112, 126, 135, 147, 156, 177, 193, 200–201, 206, 210, 221
Anti-submarine warfare carriers (ASW), 237
Arnold, General Henry H., 161
Arthur Young and Company, 47
"Assured Destruction Capability," 203, 204, 206, 208
Atherton, Howard, 101, 102
Atlas missile, 66
Atomic carriers, 60
Atomic Energy Commission, 181
Atomic-powered airplane, 59
Avco Corporation, 14, 19
Avionics systems, 60, 61, 65
AWACS air defense system, 85, 86, 87, 91, 93, 156, 206